HOW I MADE THE ANGELS CRY

{ HOW I MADE THE ANGELS CRY }

MELEISA BETTS

Neighborhood Publishing

Published by Neighborhood Publishing

Meleisa Betts
mollybetts@comcast.net
How I Made the Angels Cry
Copyright @ 2007 by Meleisa Betts

Library of Congress Cataloging-in-Publication Data
 Betts, Meleisa
 How I Made the Angels Cry/Meleisa Betts
 p. cm.
 Includes index
 ISBN13: 978-0-615-29050-8
 LCCN: 2009904080

First Neighborhood trade paperback edition April 2009.
1. Inspirational-Non-Fiction 2. Women Issues-Non-Fiction 3. Memoir-Non-Fiction 4.Devotional-Non-Fiction. I. Title

Unless otherwise noted Scripture verses are taken from the King James Version of the Bible.

All rights reserved. No part of this publication may be reproduced, stored in a retrieval system or transmittal in any form or by any means without the prior permission of the author, except for brief quotations in reviews or articles.

Cover Design: SS Media
Text and Composition: Erin New and Kim Nakiya Howard-Carswell
Edited by: Windy Goodloe

Printed in the United States of America.

THIS BOOK IS DEDICATED TO

MAZIE AND JON

Philippians 2:3

Luke 16:13

This book is a work of nonfiction, however the names, characters and places, are either the product of the author's imagination or are used fictitiously, and their resemblance, if any, to real-life counterparts is entirely coincidental. Any resemblance or references to actual events, locales, to real people, living or dead, or to real locales is coincidental.

CHAPTERS

Prologue
1

The Thousand Mile Walk
3

Where I Was When I Really Knew
11

The Undeniable Truths
22

The Trauma That Keeps On Giving
38

I Must Be A Magnet For Trouble
51

The Curse That Keeps Me Cursing
64

Blood Money
82

The Set-Up By Satan
141

It's True That When It Rains It Also Pours
176

What Can A Bad Girl Do To Be Good?
180

The Deliberation
184

Mediation
190

You Can't Outrun Your Past
194

The Prize That I Have Chased For My Entire Life
197

Looking At The Road Through The Rear-View Mirror
201

HOW I MADE THE ANGELS CRY

PROLOGUE

You know the old Native American saying, "You cannot judge a man until you have walked a mile in his moccasins." Well, I am about to take you a thousand miles in what seems like a thousand years to arrive at a story so bizarre, it will seem faked. I can assure you that everything that I am about to reveal, a baring or perhaps even a cleansing of my soul, is one hundred percent real and truthful. I hope that, through this open assessment of my life and the recent unfathomable occurrences, where the demons which seem to plague me, at times, will be vanquished, and someone who deserves it (and you know who you are) will be served the bittersweet fruit of justice. I can only try to expose this wrongdoing and hope that retribution comes to pass.

What I'm about to reveal is the honest truth in every conversation, situation, and nightmare. It is an account of a life to this point which is part nirvana and hell. It's all real. It is a story of blurred lines between homosexuality, bisexuality, heterosexuality and sexuality in general, revealing truths and the thin line between fact and fiction, and perception versus reality. Most importantly, it is a story of people and personalities, characters and character, as well as money, corruption, and murder.

I don't know what is going to happen once the truth is revealed about the evil and deprivation surrounding the person who is the antagonist of this story. I don't know if the District Attorney of the city will open an investigation into these allegations, or not. The one thing, I truly feel inside is that once I finish telling this story, it will allow the tortured soul of Phyllis, if she is in fact still earthbound, because of her unjust demise, to now cross over into the light of eternal love. The world will now know and she can finally rest in peace. "Phyllis, little T will be fine," I think as I write this memoir. Who is Phyllis? I know your inquisitive mind is asking. As the story goes, this truth will also come to light, as will the darkness of the evil that engulfed her.

{ CHAPTER 1 }

The Thousand Mile Walk

It was early spring. The rain was pouring down while the loud sound of thunder pierced my ears. I looked over to my dresser and the time on my clock read exactly 9:12 pm. It had been a little over sixty hours since I last had any sleep of significance. My eyes were dry and red. I was exhausted, but I still had a little energy in reserve. God help this poor soul of mine, I said to myself.

Earlier that afternoon, I was staring at the ceiling, and for no discernible reason, other than intuition; something told me to change my cell phone number. Even though I had just changed it the month before, I obeyed what I felt was a prompting from God, so I followed my instinct.

I called people who I thought would possibly call me over

that weekend, so they would have my new number. One of the persons I called was my old friend Madeleine, who was nicknamed Z, who was also known as Woo, for a reason that would be quite obvious if you ever met her. Woo was gorgeous, with long hair, juicy red lips, and legs that looked like they belonged on a doll. Woo was what people said when they saw her, with an exclamation, WOO!! She was a stripper who I had met at a gentleman's club some years ago. When the thunder subsided, I pick up the phone and dialed her number.

"Hello, Woo. Hey girl. What's been happening?"

"Molly, where have you been? I'm so glad you called."

"Look, girl. I'm just calling to give you my new number. I'm not gonna talk long 'cause I'm so damn tired."

"Why do you keep changing your number, child?" Woo asked.

"You already know. It's the same ol' bullshit like before."

"Not again! What the fuck happened this time?"

"I can't go into detail right now. I'll tell you 'bout it later in the week. I gotta make a couple more calls. Then I'm gonna lay my ass down."

"Girl, I know you ain't going through no more bullshit with these stupid ass hoes. Every time I talk to you, it seems like it is some kind of drama. Molly, you're damn drama queen!" Woo laughed into the receiver.

"I never talked to you 'bout it. Hell! I haven't told a lot of people 'cause the shit is so incredible that it takes so much energy to even think about it. We're talking about murder!"

"Bitch, I'm your FRIEND! You confide in friends, don't you? You and I been road dogs for eight years. I'm not good enough of a friend to share some things with? What damn murder?" she asked.

"I didn't tell you 'bout it 'cause I didn't want to drive you away. It seems as if, every time we talk, I have at least three or four dramatic situations in my life. I didn't want you to have to feel what I was feeling. You know what I'm saying? I assure you that I'll talk to you later in the week about it."

"Tomorrow is not promised. So, talk to me now. Molly, what's going on?"

"Woo, I was up all night writing out a personal synopsis of both books of Samuel from the Bible."

"A synopsis of what you read in the Bible? What in the world were you doing that for?"

I began to tell her the story of Samuel and Saul, David and Goliath, as well as Jonathan. The questions that arose in my mind were basically about how God allowed certain things to happen and why they were significant in His overall plans for the universe. The synopsis did not divulge either the how or the why of God's plan as I had hoped. Our supposed-to-be short conversation went on and on, until finally I related my insights about those biblical figures. The explanation morphed into the story of a man who had been the main antagonist in my life. I began to tell her more about my life than I had ever revealed to anyone.

"Based on what you have told me so far, I wanna know more 'bout this," Woo said, with an interest that was far from fake or staged.

"Ok, how much time you got? This story is probably gonna take all night for me to tell," I sighed.

"Just get busy talking and I'll let you know when I get tired of listening."

"I'll go back to my childhood."

"OK, I'm all ears," Woo said.

I was born in Marionville, Alabama. It was one of those hamlets that people often referred to as a one horse town.

The town had about two traffic lights, one at the beginning of Marionville and one as you were exiting. Marionville was a city of contradictions in my youth. One would think that such a small town would be a quiet and unassuming place to grow up, but Marionville was full of juicy intrigue. A great deal of that intrigue was centered on my family.

We were a family of eleven. My parents and eight other siblings were the centerpiece of the black population of Marionville. My father owned a lumber business and employed probably one third of the male population of the city. He was the prince of Marionville as his power over the black population and in some cases of the white population was clear. My daddy could do whatever he pleased in the city and this influence extended into the female population. It wasn't quite as clear to me as a child, but I later discovered that his reach into Marionville womankind was extensive.

My mother was his polar opposite, quiet and reserved. She was a stereotypical housewife, who took care of the kids. However, she assisted my father in his business to a degree. I was spoiled to a degree. My family was the envy of other families because of the things that my father could afford. I am sure that having virtually anything that I could imagine could have led to my perceptions of people with wealth yet I had no other reference point. I didn't know what it was like to want, so I could not relate to being poor. I can remember that I didn't look down on others.

One of my first memories as a child was having this thick, long, and kinky mane of hair. My mother used to straighten it with a hot comb, heated by the gas flame burners. Although it was necessary to do the hair straightening, it was uncomfortable as the heat from the stove made it seem as though it was two hundred degrees in that kitchen. First, my mother washed my hair thoroughly. She scrubbed and rubbed until my scalp was clean as could be and sometimes until it felt raw. I vaguely remember sitting on the front porch outside until it dried. I hated to get it done because it hurt like hell each and every time. The only real benefit to me physically was the pleasurable sensation that your brain feels whenever someone touched your head. Whenever mother finished my hair, it was long and beautiful, at least for a little while anyways.

However, I can clearly remember my first grade teacher, Ms. Leah. She was a pretty dark skinned lady. She would always ask me to ask my mother if she could comb my hair. I told my mother what Ms. Leah asked me and mother said yes to that innocent request. Ms. Leah would take me into the bathroom and she would comb my hair. She would tell me that I had such beautiful hair. When she finished working her magic, or so, I thought, my hair looked pretty. I didn't exactly know what was happening at the time, but I knew that the warm and soothing feeling that I felt as Ms. Leah stroked and combed my hair stirred something inside me. Mama tried, I know she did, but with being a housewife, cooking, cleaning, and making sure all the other kids were okay too, she did the best she could with my hair. Outside of the difference in the care that mama was allotted to me was the difference in how I felt when Ms. Leah attended to my kinky strands. The feeling was as opposite as getting a hug from your distant uncle, as was my feeling with mama versus the rush that you feel on Christmas morning, which was Ms. Leah.

When I got home from school every day, I would run to my room and get my favorite toy, match stems, out of their special hiding place. They were something, that for no apparent reason, I had an obsession over. But looking back, it could have had everything to do with my personality trait of trying to make something out of literally nothing. I kept them in a secret place because I knew that my daddy, who was a stern disciplinarian, didn't want me in my room playing with them. I would play for hours at a time, with the burned matches, using what most people would consider rubbish to amuse myself. Mama never said anything to me at all about this.

At that time, daddy was smoking cigars and mama was smoking cigarettes. So, there was always a ready supply of the inexpensive objects of my affection. It wasn't the fire aspect of matches as much as what my imagination could use the singed little wooden sticks for. My parents used the hard wooden matches that came in a square box. Whenever they threw one away, I would run and get it. In my inventive mind, I would recreate it as a man or woman. The ones which burned real low were the children. The ones that burned to the quick at the round top were men with very little hair. The ones that burned a little and were quickly extinguished were women with long hair. For some reason, I would always imagine them to be beautiful. Although all the matches smelled of sulfur, I imagined that the smell would be attributed to the male matchsticks; while, the female sticks had the fragrance of perfume. The boxes that contained the matches were the cars. Sometimes, I would put them together as if it was a family and that would be the family's vehicle.

I would play with my toys, from 3:15 in the afternoon from the moment that I got off of the school bus, until daddy came home at around 5 or 6 PM. My mother would have his food on the table like clockwork. I could hear daddy's voice shouting, "Where's Molly? Is she back there with them damn matches?" Even today, in my mind, I can hear him again screaming, "Molly, get your ass out that room!"

I would politely put the matchsticks away. I hid them as well as I could from daddy, given the circumstances. I knew that when I wasn't inside the house, he was trying to find them, but try as he might, he never could. My parents eventually bought me Barbie and Ken dolls and an action figure named "Big Jim" for my birthdays and Christmas. I would take them into my inner sanctuary and invariably pretended they were having sex. Yes, I did know what sex was as a seven year-old, but I was a little fuzzy about the mechanics. Eventually, I grew tired of the match stems and I fell totally in love with the little dolls. Big Jim ended up breaking his rubberized plastic legs, so I unceremoniously buried him in the back yard. They all eventually ended up losing a body part or two, so I just buried them, too. Maybe this ritual meant something, since I wouldn't just throw them into the trash. I had to entomb them as though they were actually flesh and blood that was being returned to its origins.

My mind went from fancying items such as movie projectors to pianos, to whatever drew my attention. Eventually I would receive whatever it was that was the object of my desire, usually more sooner than later. I had everything that a girl could want. I didn't really realize how fortunate I was at the time. However, this act by my parents of fulfilling my every whim may have set the stage for my life. In fact, I am sure that it had a great influence.

I kept to myself most of the time as a child. I was always interested in what I could do or create. I was a bit weird, I would have to admit. I loved television almost as much as my dolls and matchsticks. We had one television and it had only two channels that could be received in our area. Whenever one channel became fuzzy, regardless of the weather conditions, one of us would have to go outside and turn the antenna, regardless of the outside conditions. If we woke daddy up during the commotion, we had to turn the television off. It didn't matter if we were in the middle of a good movie or whatever the case may have been. If he had to tell us to turn the television off more than once, we were in big trouble; maybe a whipping with his belt would have been the order of the moment. There was no such thing as a "time out" at the time.

Once my doll obsession ended, I then moved on to music as my focus. I remember one instance when I had my music playing in my room. I had a big stereo set with a record player, a radio, and an eight track player. I would forget and leave it on whenever I went outside. Now I had started to be more sociable rather than solitary, such as going outside to watch my brothers, Blake and Carlton, wash their motorcycles or play basketball with their friends. There were so many people playing ball or just goofing off. It was a lot of fun as opposed to my previously hermetic lifestyle.

One day, I forgot to turn off my stereo. Daddy had warned me before not to leave it playing while I was not in the house. When I came back inside, daddy had gotten a knife and cut the cord to my stereo. When he cut the cord, he dropped the end that was connected to the power outlet, so the frayed wires started a fire on the curtains in my room. Daddy managed to put the blaze out before the whole house caught on fire. He took the cord and plug out of the outlet and kept it, to keep me from taping the wires back together and using the stereo once more. I was so sad. I went to tell mama, and she just shook her head. I can only guess that right there was the moment that I figured out that, cutting cords was like cutting ties with people. Sometimes you need to patch the rift in order to keep the music going, sometimes you just cannot repair the rift, and sometimes the heat from the destroyed part is great enough to burn or injure you. I guess it's true that life is a lesson.

{ CHAPTER 2 }

Where I Was When I Really Knew

I remember in the fourth grade, I had a white female teacher named Mrs. Wallace. Every day, I would gaze at her because I had fallen in love. I was as in love with Ms. Wallace as any eight year-old could be with a woman who was probably twenty years older than me. I made it a point to do whatever it took to be in her presence. If it was cleaning erasers or asking her questions, whatever it took I did it. In my childishly love-struck mind, it didn't really matter that society said that girls should like boys. If I could have found a way to have married the married Mrs. Wallace, I would have. I was an eight year old girl who was fully aware that I was in love with a woman! She was gorgeous. She had luminous bluish-gray eyes that seemed too beautiful to be real, long brunette hair, a flawless complexion and lips that were constantly thick with red lipstick. I also knew that there were complete female opposites of my fascination with Mrs. Wallace.

I can remember being in the sixth grade, while I was playing outside during physical education class. I was way out from the rest of the class. I guess I was too far away from my teacher. This white female for whom I didn't have a Mrs. Wallace-type affinity, sent another student to tell me to come back closer to the rest of the class. The fact that I can't remember her name speaks volumes.

"The teacher said that you are too far and you need to come closer."

"Tell her that I said to go to hell."

I really didn't mean that. I don't really know why she ran and told the teacher exactly what I said, other than to get me into trouble. I was called to the principal's office because of my statement. The teacher and the principal, Mr. Riley, who was a light-skinned drunk, called my mother and told her what I had said. She had to come to the school with me the next day or I would be suspended.

When I got home, I told my mother what had happened. She agreed that what was said was between two children and that the girl didn't have to go back to the teacher with that comment. She also agreed that it was clear that the girl was trying to get me into trouble. It wasn't quite clear to me then, but in looking back on that time, I was formulating my opinion that it wasn't just women, but the kindness in them, that I was most attracted to. In my pre-adolescent mind, Mr. Riley was just a vile figurehead who may have in part impacted some of my opinions of men. The white teacher, though not unattractive, seemed to view me as more of an inconvenient nuisance than a student. So, my affinity for her was about the same as my feelings for Riley. In short, I wasn't just attracted to all women but to the ones who were kind and compassionate. I didn't always follow that paradigm in later life, but for the most part I did. While driving home from school, I looked over at mama and I began to cry and plead.

"Mama, please don't tell daddy!"

"I won't, baby, but you must not use those types of words anymore."

"I won't mama, I promise."

I knew that he would beat the hell out of me. She didn't say a word to him about my brush with suspension and I was so glad. I think in many ways, my mother was my model of what was worthy and noble about womanhood. Quiet but strong, soft, beautiful, and feminine. Through her I realized, not only what I wanted, but what I didn't want in either friends or relationships. I wanted someone who would keep my confidence and best interest at heart and shun those who tried to harm or use me. She was my angel in my life that gave me direction by her actions; and only if I had paid closer attention, I could have saved myself some future heartache. As the saying goes, hindsight is always 20/20 vision.

There is a tremendously erroneous myth about the ability of a person to will or talk themselves out of their sexual orientation. Some religious figures talk about the "demon" of homosexuality. The reality is that the choice of whether or not one chooses to gravitate toward men or women is inherent. It is a feeling, desire, or affinity that is inborn. I knew very early in my life that I found women fascinating. I loved the softness of women, how they had a fragrance that was vastly different than that of men; even when they were musky with the scent of effort and perspiration. It was no more of a choice for me to like women than it was for me to decide whether or not I would be born with a penis or a vagina. Who would choose a sexual orientation that would cause instant vilification by society? One would be an absolute idiot to make such a choice. I didn't know what my sexual orientation was at age seven, eight, or nine year-old. But, I could tell as early as I could remember that I was the most happiest in the presence of women.

"So, you pretty much knew that you were a lesbian by the time you were about eight or nine years old?" Woo asked.

"I didn't know that much, but I did know that I loved women more than in a casual way. At that time, in the early seventies, there was no talk of lesbians. They were called bull daggers. These were rough, manly looking women who had their own girlfriends. I can't remember more than one or two women who were clearly "out" during that time in Marionville. Of course, I wouldn't identify with them in that regard. The fact that I liked females was just, you know, like a natural thing to me," I said.

"I got ya. Just like how I knew that I liked boys. I didn't know how to have sex at eight or nine, but I knew that my sexuality was pointed in the direction of males. I can see that clearly," Woo said.

"See, one of the problems is that most of the time, no one is one hundred percent of anything. The Kinsey Report on sexuality said something like that. Sort of like on a scale of zero to one hundred, a man or woman, depending on what you are measuring, is either absolutely or degrees of something on that scale," I said. .

"I don't quite follow you. Please elaborate," Woo said.

I replied, "Okay, say the scale is measuring homosexuality. A man or woman who is completely heterosexual is a zero, meaning that they have no desires or inclinations toward the opposite sex. The thought of being with someone of their same sex is sickening to them. On the other end of the scale is the one hundred percent homosexual man or woman. Many women who are completely homosexual have never ever been penetrated by a penis and find that act revolting. They are "virgins" forever. The one hundred percent homosexual man is the same. They have never been with or desired women. All of their sexuality is geared toward men. Then you have degrees of how much someone is or isn't in terms of sexuality. For example, I am probably eighty percent homosexual since I have slept with men. I do find qualities in them that are appealing. Don't get it twisted, though. Just because I'm not repulsed by them, doesn't mean that I have to have them. I crave women and that is the difference. Another example is that a man who is ninety percent heterosexual could find himself attracted to a transsexual who looks like a woman. That ten percent of him that would have sex with a man disguised as a woman is why he isn't considered one hundred percent heterosexual. Does that make sense to you?" I asked.

"It makes perfect sense. I guess that in an extreme case, if no men were around, I could be physically attracted to a woman who looked very much like a man and have sex with her, but she would have to look like Denzel Washington," Woo joked.

We both laughed at that comment for about a minute. Then I resumed.

"See, I hear people use terms like bisexuality for anyone who can have sex with either gender. I think that it is bullshit. It's like Richard Pryor once said 'either you suck dicks or you don't.' That's the truth. I am a lesbian who doesn't mind having sex with men on occasion, but I am still a homosexual. I'm not split down the middle fifty-fifty and I believe that most people aren't. There are probably some people in the world who are split in their sexuality, if you go by the sliding scale theory. In the vast majority of cases, the person is either heterosexual or homosexual from birth. The question is whether or not they are completely one way or another and then how close to that one hundred percent figure are they," I said.

"Wow, man, you summed that up better than these people that come on talk shows and pretend that they know what's up. That's some deep shit," Woo said.

"I'm just keeping it real. I am a lesbian. I was born this way. I didn't choose this feeling. It more or less chose me. I'm not ashamed of it because my sexuality is just a part of who I am. Why lie 'bout it or sugarcoat things? I am a homosexual who likes women, not a bisexual, or any other label that misleads someone," I said.

"Okay, thanks for the lesson on sexuality, Dr. Molly. You may now resume your story," Woo quipped.

****

There always seemed to be a dark cloud over me that took years for me to come to terms with and quantify. Even though I had everything that a girl could ask for in terms of material trappings, for the most part, my social interactions were more introverted than gregariously extroverted, which I longed to be. That would come later in life, but at that time, darkness persisted and sad times prevailed, even to the point that at ten years of age, I tried to kill myself. Fortunately for me, I was not skilled in the art of self-poisoning. I took twenty antibiotic capsules in order to perform the deed. I had no idea that all I did was prevent myself from catching a cold or bolster my defenses against infection.

My mother had to get permission from daddy to drive

the prized family car, a Cadillac, to my school the next day. Usually she wasn't allowed to drive it. Only daddy drove it while she sat in the passenger's seat, almost like it was a ritual of sorts. He would hide the keys to the car in his office, so that she couldn't sneak and drive his prized automobile. I never completely understood their dynamic, but I believe that daddy knew that my mother was beautiful and he wanted to control her movement, either at the house or in general. He figured that a woman's place was the age-old belief of cooking, cleaning, and having babies.

I'm sure that my daddy's opinions of women also shaped my view of men, somewhat. This belief, if my assumptions were correct, seemed in opposition to what I felt as a female. The contradiction was that he, as well as many other men that had lived for thousands of years, shared the image in their psyche, of a woman being barefoot and pregnant, despite the fact that they were running around cavorting with other women. My father was certainly guilty of this double standard as he would be cheating on my mother with a cavalcade of women, while his workers were in the woods doing their jobs. It was more than okay for him to have both his slice of the proverbial cake and mother's cake too. He would have been incensed if my mother had done to him what he had done to her.

We all met at the principal's office that day and I apologized to the teacher and that was that. It was over and daddy never knew a word of it. To this day, I probably value trust and confidentiality in my relationships more than any other attribute because of my mother.

I visited my grandmother every weekend. I loved my grandma. Her name was Lenora. I often wondered why she had an outhouse, a wood stove, and a fire place when indoor plumbing was prevalent everywhere. Maybe it was because she was simple country folk. That explanation was more than enough for me. My older sister, Rebeca, lived with Grandma Lenora at the time. After I was much older, I asked my mama why Rebeca stayed with Grandma.

Mama said, "Rebeca doesn't remember this, because she was young at the time, but she asked me if she could stay with Grandma because she wanted all her toys to herself."

During the 60's, daddy wasn't doing as well financially. My oldest sisters and brothers didn't have it as well, but Rebeca had her own big ass humongous playhouse on the side of grandma's house. It was filled with toys and a big blue bicycle. The playhouse was bigger than a bedroom in some houses which seemed a curious combination, given the stone-age surroundings of my grandma. Our breakfast ritual was to have yellow grits at Grandma Lenora's house in the mornings. She cooked all of our food under a fire, even in the sweltering heat of summer.

We took baths in a small bowl which took the place of the large tubs we were accustomed to. We were not terribly inconvenienced by doing so. We got our drinking water and bathing water from a pump in the backyard. The water was always surprisingly good and cold, even during the dog days of August. I used to wonder why daddy didn't help grandma fix her house up since his financial position improved later.

I asked mother, "Why daddy won't help grandma?"

Mama replied, "I asked daddy to help my mother, and he flatly said no. I told him if you can't help my mother with nothing then you will not be helping your parents."

In her mind, it was right for right and wrong for wrong which equaled fair treatment. She said that she meant just what she said. Sadly, neither of the relatives on either side received any help from our family as per that edict.

Grandma Lenora passed away when I was ten years old. Two months after she had passed away, I saw her sitting on my mother's bed looking at me. I believed she appeared because earlier that evening I had snuck over to my brother-in-law's party that was going on next door to us. I secretly tasted some beer. I knew that I had no business doing that being a child, although a precocious one. Honestly, in looking back that alcohol could have factored into my vision, but I would see things despite the alcohol. I had been having such visions for as long as I could remember.

At Grandma's funeral, I didn't sit in the front; rather I sat at the back of the church because I didn't want to see Grandma. I was hurt, but I was scared of dead people. I have been scared every since I was old enough to know what it meant to pass away. Probably because at that point, I understood that what I was seeing was earthbound spirits. I never slept with the lights off; even today, I have to have the room lit. The only time I sleep with the lights off is when someone is staying the night with me and sleeping in the same bed.

My mother told me that when I was born, there was a "veil" over my face, which is a thin membrane. There is a belief in the black community that when a child is born with a veil that he or she has "the shine". The shine is an ability to see spirits, and I have seen many since childhood. Some of the spirits will occasionally make themselves apparent to me in the daylight. They usually occur when the lights in the room are either dimmed to near darkness or when it is total darkness. It is frightening to me to turn out the lights in a room, as the cavalcade of spirits will begin to cascade back and forth through the room.

My mother's uncle had a stroke. He was in Selma, Alabama

when it happened, so mama drove to the hospital and brought him to our home.

As soon as daddy got home I heard him say, "He can't stay here."

Mama had to put Uncle Sun in a nursing home in Marionville. She reiterated to daddy as before that "if none of my people can stay here, none of your people will stay here." Since her uncle, who really needed help, was turned away, then everyone, whether immediate family or distant, would be turned away also. She was just a person that believed in treating people the same regardless of status.

I guess this is why my Granddaddy Jake, my daddy's father, never lived with us after his wife, Grandma Mozell, passed away. Eventually, he became much too old to continue caring for himself. He had to live with his other sons at one time or another but never with us. I never had the close relationship that I wish I had with Granddaddy Jake. Unfortunately, I was too young to remember the details behind Grandmamma Mozell's passing, yet I could remember her being very sick. As I mentally fast-forward to the time when I was about seventeen years of age, Granddaddy Jake had begun to come by to see daddy a lot, each time with one of his other sons. When he came to visit my dad, and after a little while of sitting on the porch, he would say, "Molly, come on here and take me for a ride."

I would always say, "Ok, granddaddy."

The thing is that I never did nor did I ever stop by whichever uncle's house he was living with at the time to pick him up and take him for a ride. I could have easily done so but for no reason that I can fathom, I never did. Some days I passed right by Uncle Will's, where he had spent the majority of his later years. Uncle Will and granddaddy would be sitting right out on the front porch of the house, as big as the sun, and I would blow my horn and keep on trucking. I have lived with that regret everyday of my life for some odd reason, be it from guilt, remorse or for some reason that I will never know. But as I recollect to that particular part of my past, it was at that time in my life, where I focused on women in almost every aspect of my awareness and waking thoughts. My obsession with all things female was to the point where I probably shortchanged the male figures in my life, particularly Granddaddy Jake. Once again I ponder how these relationships, or lack of them, have shaped my sensibilities and affected my Karma, if they have at all. The thing that I am convinced of is that my father's self-centeredness may have caused me to miss out on some of my family spending their golden years with us and the stories that they may have held. My self-centeredness at that time was a direct reflection on what I had seen in my father.

****

{ CHAPTER 3 }

The Undeniable Truths

Here I was an attractive, thirteen year old fox, when this crazy ass white boy and a black boy came running—racing along the sidewalk. They ran slap over me as if I wasn't standing there at all. The result of the collision was that my entire chin was skinned and raw for months until it finally healed. That incident didn't help my opinion of boys, who I thought were generally stupid and stinky like any pubescent girl would or should. I knew that it was dictated by society for me to like boys, but my subconscious was drawing the inference "You see Molly, those boys will only be trouble and pain; a sweet and soft woman could never hurt you that way." I was not anti-males at that point by a long shot but it was starting to become clearer to me, more than at any other time, that I vastly preferred women. However, there was no real outlet for my desires for women until a little later, a year later to be precise. At that particular time, I could only fantasize about females until an opportunity to act on my desires came to fruition.

It was around that same point in time when I became aware that my daddy had illicit, but somewhat widely known among the local people, relationships within a family that had seven sisters, the Stanfordson girls. I guess you could call my daddy a player, since eventually he had twenty or so women who were stupid enough to all be seeing him. Maybe they were just a bunch of stupid whores, plain and simple. I guess I chose to go with the stupid hoe assessment. I will have to admit that my father did have the qualities most women desired. He was tall, dark, handsome, and was well off or in the vernacular "he was paid."

At the time he was dating Jene Stanfordson, the older and heaviest of the very attractive Stanfordson women. Jene didn't like my mama one bit. This was the dynamic that I could never figure out, because Jene was the adulterer not the victim. It should be noted that all the women in that family were absolutely gorgeous and the men were handsome as hell. Their mother was a little white woman and their father was tall, real dark and handsome as my dad was tall, dark and handsome. Outside of the fact that my mother was not white, there were similarities between our two warring factions. In my mind, none of the animosity as well as the relationships made any sense.

Jene's husband worked for my dad as a saw man, in my father's lumber company. Jene controlled virtually everything that Black ass Rat ever did, which ironically was his name as far as we all knew. She told him when to eat, sleep, work, fuck, and everything in between. Black ass Rat knew that Jene was sleeping with my daddy, but apparently a job was more important than self- esteem; knowing that your boss was screwing your wife. All the husbands of the sisters knew about their wives sleeping with my dad. None of them did a damn thing about stopping it. He had them all paralyzed to act against him, because if they pissed him off, they could easily be found homeless and trying to find a way to fill the empty bellies of their wives and children. It was a cold-blooded Catch-22 situation, which they were more or less stuck into accepting.

Jene coerced her two youngest sisters, Belenda and Dorothy, to jump on me and beat me up after school, maybe out of spite and hatred over my mother. I had heard they were going to fight me the night before through my friend Sherry. She told me what she heard, so I was prepared for them with a knife pick that I had hidden in my book bag the night before. I was dating a guy named Donnie at the time. He was the first male I had actually decided to "go with" at the age of thirteen. I still knew that I really desired girls, but paradoxically I was in love with Donnie as much as my budding, but sexually conflicted thirteen year old mind could comprehend loving a male. Yes, in retrospect, if truth be told, Belenda Stanfordson was in love with him, too. In actuality, she may have been in love with Donnie, whereas I was going through the phase of doing what I was supposed to do as dictated by society.

The next day, Belenda and her sister Dorothy were standing at the bus stop. Dorothy had gone over to Donnie's motorcycle, which was parked outside of the school, and took his helmet off of the handlebar. She had it in her hand. It was clear that she was going to use it on me. They were waiting to assault me. All the while, they were talking big shit. I had my little green bag on my shoulder with my hand inside on the red ice pick ready to inflict some major hurt on those two heifers. I had gotten the ice pick out of my mother's drawer the night before. She had won that ice pick at the fair that came to town once a year. No one ever questioned what an odd as hell prize an ice pick was for winning anything. I told mother nothing about what Sherry had told me.

When Belenda and Dorothy started talking about what they were planning to do to me, I just stood there eyeing the both of them. Belenda suddenly pushed me. Then I pulled out the ice pick and stuck it in her right arm. The bitch started crying and bleeding. A split second later, I felt a blow to my head. Dorothy had hit me with the motorcycle helmet. She used it as a weapon, just as I had surmised.

I fell to the concrete pavement. Dorothy then jumped on top of me and pulled my hair. All I could hear was her screaming, "You done stab my sister!" In what seemed like seconds later, Mr. Joe, my favorite bus driver, and another bus driver snatched Dorothy off of me. They came to my rescue like black knights in shining armor. Mr. Joe put me on the bus and then retrieved his baseball bat from out of the bus and put an end to the lopsided affair once and for all. You see, the Stanfordson family was known in all the surrounding areas for jumping on people. They jumped on you in groups. They kicked your doors down. They beat asses and didn't call names. The women in that family were such fighters that they were known for whipping their husband's asses.

This was a new day for me, because they'd really beat my ass, even though I had stabbed Belenda. However, the truth is that only God, my mother, and my cousin Diane knew that when Dorothy hit me on the head with that helmet, I lost my bladder and peed on myself. It was a good thing that no one could see it because my green nylon pants camouflaged the stain of the accident. The incident happened in front of virtually the whole population of our small hamlet. It stood to reason that the entire town knew about it. The news spread like wildfire all over Marionville, Alabama. People were so happy to see me when we went to town. Although for the sake of self-consciousness, I didn't come back to town until after the plug of hair I lost during the fight had grown back on the top of my head. I wore a cap for months.

Everybody was saying, we are so glad you beat that girl. They go for bad, but you showed her. I didn't say anything. I knew that they were basing their judgment on who won or lost on the stabbing. They didn't know about my loss of bladder control or the plug of my hair taking nearly two months in which to grow back. They didn't see the bruises all over my body that those bitches managed to inflict. Even to this day, I have these headaches all the time because of the vicious blow to my head.

Even though I was not the aggressor and was only defending myself like anyone else would, I was kicked out of school for the remaining of the school year. Those evil monsters, Dorothy and Belenda, were allowed to stay. My mother got the keys to the Cadillac from my daddy. He didn't say one damn word because he knew that this mess was because of Jene Stanfordson. My mother drove me to another school in another county school called Fitchburg High. I went to school every day. My mother told me not to tell them anything, if someone asked me why I was there. I didn't say one word. I so enjoyed the kids there. I wouldn't know them if I saw them today, but they were all so sweet.

At the end of the school year, I tried to re-enroll in my former high school. I was told by Marion County high officials that they could not accept my grades from another school because I had been expelled from Marion County. I was not eligible to be in any school for the rest of that year. Because of this ass-backwards decision, I had to go to summer school to make up my grades. The Stanfordson sisters were probably fucking the principal for him to come up with that decision. Although that was just another example of my wild imagination at work, I'm sure.

They sure as hell were fucking the deputy sheriff of the county. This was alleged among the people of the town. His name was Auther Roy, Sr.; and they made no bones about screwing him at all. In fact, he pompously came to our house the afternoon right after the incident happened to try and serve me a warrant. My oldest brother Sol stood up and said, "You go tell them, if they take out a warrant against Molly, we will take one out against Belenda and Dorothy."

Auther quickly jumped into his sheriff's car and zoomed down to Limestone Drive to tell Jene what Sol had barked to him. My daddy was sitting right there in the garage as all of this unfolded. He never opened his mouth, probably because he had a somewhat twisted, conflict of interest, seeing as how he was plowing Jene on a regular basis. Despite all of the fuss and hoopla, we never heard any thing else from the warrant.

My mother told my daddy, "You better tell your women that they can have your black ass, but they better not mess with my children!" She basically told him he had better put his whore's ass in check. He did so after that, I sometimes wonder if these incidents with all of the conflicted emotions and subtexts have made an indelible impression on my consciousness. Maybe it may have warped my perception of life and sexuality in some abstract way. Oh, well, if that is the case, then I can only do the best I can with what I'm left with.

****

"Dang, girl! You had a lot of shit going on in just a few years of life. You had all these crushes on women and your daddy was a straight-up pimp daddy, and all kinds of stuff. It seems like you're thirteen going on thirty with all of this crap going on in your life. You needed me back then 'cause we woulda whupped them bitches' asses," Woo said.

I responded, " I'm just beginning. There is a hell of a lot left to this story. Really, you've just heard the tame shit. I ain't even told you the R- and X- rated shit, yet."

"Go on, I'm listening."

As I grew into my teenage sexuality, I developed friends that at first I liked to indulge in innocuous activities with such as kissing and what black people called "hunching" and some white people refer to as "dry humping". At the age of fourteen, I fell in love with this pretty girl who moved to Marionville from Indiana. Her name was Vickie. She was the granddaughter of a town resident named Sam Gregg. My daddy was also involved sexually with Mr. Gregg's wife. He had all the women in Marionville under his spell. Sam knew it, but he just resigned himself to it as did all of the other men in town. Vickie was beautiful. I had to get the word to her in some way in order to gauge her interest. I persuaded my best friend, Eldrin, to tell Vickie how I felt about her and he did.

Eldrin wrote a note and passed it to Vickie. Molly likes you.

She wrote back to him. I know that she likes me.

Then Eldrin wrote back to her. No, she likes you like a guy likes a girl.

I watched her reactions closely. She sat at her desk without looking at either of us. After a minute or so, she finally reacted. First, she laughed and couldn't stop laughing. She was giggling about my proposal and she couldn't wait for the end of class to blab it to her gossipy cousin, Tori. Once she did this, that note became THE topic at the school. It spread that, Molly is a bull dagger. Bull dagger is the black folk's version of what whites call a bull dike, meaning that I was the "male" version of a lesbian. Hell, I didn't care because my declaration must have worked. Vickie eventually started liking me. This is the way that our relationship began:

One afternoon, after school, I invited Tori and Vickie over to my house. They accepted.

I asked Vickie, "Can I kiss you?"

She answered with an emphatic, "NO!"

However, Tori encouraged Vickie to kiss me, so she finally relented. Vickie's lips were soft and moist but it was clear to me that she had not kissed many boys, if any at all. However, I could feel that Vickie was enjoying her first lesbian kiss immensely. I held her at the small of her back as would a man as my tongue danced with hers. We kissed for at least a minute. She suddenly broke away from me, saying she was upset and that she wanted to go home. They left, but I called her that night and we talked for hours. Eventually, we could not go a day without talking to or being with each other. We started riding together in my El Camino. We sometimes talked on the phone all night. We kissed, hunched, and just generally enjoying each other. Neither one of us knew about oral sex at that time, but we knew that we had a strong physical attraction for each other.

"Stop right there, girl. You were riding in your what?" Woo asked.

"My El Camino. I know that you are wondering how in the hell did a fourteen year-old manage that, but I'll get to that. Trust me."

"Pardon the interruption then. You may proceed," Woo

said.

Mrs. Gregg, Sam's wife, got wind of our relationship and she sent Vickie back to Indiana post haste. I cried over the loss of my beloved Vickie and so did she over me. We were madly in love with each other by that time. To be quite honest, she was my first true love. Even today we still communicate, despite the fact that it has been more than twenty eight years. It's been about six years since I last saw her. She was still pretty then, too. From what I understand from people that know her, she is still a beautiful young lady with long straight hair, light skinned, pretty teeth, and a nice body, all qualities that men, as well as some women like myself, covet.

Around the age of eighteen, five years after I had lost my virginity to a man, was when I did the actual deed of consensual man and woman intercourse for the second time. This time it with a young black man named Lance, who I met. He was a member of the infamous Stanfordson family. He and I fucked because I had heard that Lance had a big dick. I had to find out for myself if this was true. He damn sure did! We had sex in my car in the parking lots of several places, some private and some public.

I only did it to get back at his family who thought that they were so much more than my family. Besides, they had been tormenting my mother by screwing my father. So, I thought it right to return the favor. How in the hell could they figure that they were above us in stature was beyond me. Because we were the shit family in Marionville, at least as far as black people and my perception went. My reasons may have been fucked up, but that was my rationale.

Somewhere in the midst of my encounter with Lance, I pretty much came to the conclusion that, although sex with a man was not disgusting, it was something I could take or leave;

like eating a bologna sandwich versus having a nice steak dinner at Bones, no pun intended. Three years after that experience, at the age of twenty one, I moved to West Palm Beach, Florida. I would drive back home at least once a month. On one of those weekend trips, I happened to begin having some rather risqué and racy conversations with Sonya Stanfordson. Sonya was Jene Stanfordson sister and Belenda Stanfordson's aunt. Sonya was the prettiest of them all by far. She had sandy colored hair, beautiful teeth, smooth skin, and the body to go with it. She had a soft, sweet voice. Sonya was drop dead gorgeous!!!

By this time my sexual desires were geared toward women and to the nearly virtual exclusion of men. It was still difficult to have labeled myself totally lesbian at that point. Since I was involved with men to a small degree, I was probably more on the lesbian side of the fence than anything. Again, I did not find men and the act of intercourse disgusting rather I found women beautiful and I enjoyed the emotional kinship that we shared. Sonya and I started fucking every time I drove home to visit my mother. The wild card in this situation was the fact that Sonya too was married!

The point to this was that not only had I experienced both a heterosexual and a homosexual relationship. Within a three year period, it was between a male and a female within a family which by all rights, because of my past with them, I should have been at war with, instead of having sex with them. Incredibly, I even had a sexual tryst with Belenda Stanfordson, the same Belenda who had jumped me along with her sister Dorothy back when we were thirteen. The same Belenda who I had stabbed in her arm with an ice pick! Belenda and I ended up in my car, as did Sonya, kissing fondling, and hunching. I cannot explain this intense series of events with the Stanfordson family, except to hypothesize, that hate and love are strong emotions. Both are passionate responses in their intensity and just maybe there was a lot of sexual tension between our families. Whatever the case, I seemed to be screwing a lot with a family of which I should be mortal enemies.

The sanctity of marriage was an arbitrary concept in my hometown of Marionville. The Stanfordson women took their vows of chastity and faithfulness as no more than a formality. It seemed now that as a subtext to it all was that I wanted to get back at the Stanfordson family. First through Lance, and three years later, through Sonya and Belenda, for having caused my mother so much pain, because of the Stanfordson women's adultery with my father. Ironically, Sonya had also been intimately involved with my daddy at one time. So in this regard, my father and I had crossed paths sexually as it were.

It was difficult to describe my situation at that point. At the time that I was screwing with Sonya, I had a boyfriend in West Palm Beach, Florida. His name was Andrew Brewington. He was a well-to-do, very much older gentleman. He was far more infatuated with me than I was with him, obviously; yet, our relationship was not sexually oriented in the least. That he liked the way I looked was the probable reason that we were together. As long as he was keeping me financially situated, that was enough for me at that time. I am sure that most of my relationships with men stemmed from financial reasons, but my dealings with women were predominantly based on desire. To that end, Sonya and I would meet practically every other weekend and be intimate in the back seat of Andrew Brewington's Rolls Royce. He trustingly let me drive it home to parade it in front of the hometown folks. I thought, because I was driving a one hundred thousand dollar vehicle, I was the shit for real!

Sonya fucked up in 1990 at my brother-in-law's funeral. I had told her before that my parents could never know about us and she agreed. She came up to me with her stupid oblivious-to-the-truth husband while we all were standing outside. She tried to begin a conversation with me, which to me seemed to telegraph the nature of our relationship to whomever that had any amount of common sense. I walked off and tried to act unemotional because I knew mama was looking. I tried to appear as if I didn't know her and this was our first conversation.

The next day mama asked me, "Baby, are you friends with Sonya?"

I said, "No!" It was almost a defiant shout rather than a rational reaction. My protesting probably gave me away more than anything in mama's eyes.

This was the first and only lie that I ever told mama. I never told her the truth about Sonya.

She said, "Well, Sonya's husband told daddy that you were friends with her and that you come by and picked up Sonya all the time."

I said in a loud voice, "MAMA, SHE IS LYING!"

Mama didn't say anything. She stared at me with cold eyes that had the look of someone with the sadness of betrayal; I truly believe she knew that I was lying, but she never asked me again. After that incident, I completely cut my ties with Sonya forever. When she called, I never answered. I never dialed her number again in life.

****

"I got a question for you, Molly. All I ever see you with or hear you talking 'bout is these light- skinned or mixed-race people. Were those chicks, Sonya and Belenda, light-skinned, too?" Woo asked, with a hint of 'I know the answer already' to the tone of her voice.

"Yup, she was light-complexioned. I thought I mentioned that earlier. Were you not listening, Missy? I've been involved with dark-skinned women. In fact, that old saying "the blacker the berry the sweeter the juice" is true. That shit is sho- nuff the truth," I said.

"How's that? Pussy is pussy," Woo said flatly.

I responded, "There is a difference and you just have to either experience it or just take my word for it. Hell, there's a difference between black and white women and black and white men. Maybe it's the chemistry of the different kinds of people, but that difference is real. Just like the myth of black men having big dicks and white men having small ones. That is pure bullshit!" I said, knowing that the volume of my voice could probably be heard in the hallway of my condominium.

"Yeah girl, that is a crock of shit 'bout that dick thang. Hell, I've dated white men with big fat dicks and brothers with little ding dings," Woo laughed hysterically at her own comment.

I said, "All I know is that it's been my experience with different women, that real dark women have the best pussy. It tastes better and they are always extra wet for some reason. Just like the difference in when a black man ejaculates and when a white man does it. Maybe it is the chemical makeup of the two men, but the scent is stronger with a black man and it lingers with you longer."

"I don't know if I go along with you on that one," Woo responded.

"Ok, you ever go past a stall where a black woman has been and smelled a strong odor?" I asked.

"Yeah, sometimes I have."

"What about when a white woman has been there first? You recall any lingering scent?" I asked.

"No. Not that I can recall. What's your point?"

I said, "The point is that if a black woman carries that strong-ass semen in her from that black man for one day it's gonna smell. A black man's ejaculation smells stronger than a white man's. This is just my experience. It's just a theory. I'm not trying to be prejudiced against my own race of people."

"Girl, white or black, an ass is an ass! I'm a sister, but I don't buy into that semen theory at all. So, you just go on with this damn crazy-ass story of yours. This shit is like part comedy, tragedy, murder mystery, and drama wrapped up in one big fucking package," Woo joked.

"Yup, I'm hoping that Phyllis's murderer is brought to justice." That was my only response, since she was right.

"What? What murder?"

"I'll get to that, but first let me get back to my childhood story," I stated.

I remember this story just as if it is happening right now. One afternoon, someone called mama on the phone and told her something she obviously didn't like, as evidenced by the scowl on her face. She hung up and went to her drawer, got her little .22 Pistol and said, "Come on, baby." She knew how to get into daddy's office and she got the keys to daddy's precious Cadillac. It was very clear that daddy wasn't very good at hiding things. On many occasions, my mother sneaked into the office, got those keys to the car and we would just joyride around Marionville. She knew that one of daddy's women would probably tell him if they saw her, but she really didn't care. Once we got into town, mama parked the car in front of Lee Motors, the local car lot. She had me by the one hand

and the pistol in the other while we crossed the street. She wasn't looking in any direction but straight ahead. I was looking right at her all the while. We almost got hit by a car while crossing the street, she was so focused.

The sound of the horn blowing from the car that almost hit us alerted daddy and Jene. They were together in the car lot talking with a salesman. They fled before mama could get all the way across the street. The phone call was probably someone alerting mama that daddy was getting ready to buy Jene a new car. That plan was put on hold forever as the transaction never happened. To this day, I believe that Aunt Rock, my daddy's sister, called my mother. She and my mother were extremely close. My mother loved Aunt Rock, whose real name was actually Rocksie Anne. Aunt Rock would come by the house and she would curse with every word that came out of her mouth. She would have mama laughing and so would I.

I would be listening to 'grown folks business.' I wasn't leaving mama's side for anybody and she never tried to make me. I never kept any secrets from her other than the Sonya Stanfordson affair and she never kept any from me, at least as far as I had ever known. I learned a good lesson from mama and her informant. It was important to have eyes in high and low places.

****

"So, you were a hot little mama back then, huh?" Woo said.

I said, "That little shit ain't nothing. You're 'bout to hear some real deep shit about me, something that only me and my family knows. Hell, I may as well tell you the whole story since I've gone this far. This ain't no weak shit. So you better be sure that you're ready for it."

"You ain't scaring me, bitch, with those threats! I wanna see if this shit is as strong as you claim. Go ahead, let's see what you got, trick!" Woo joked.

"Be careful what you ask for," I warned. I should start heeding my own advice.

{ CHAPTER 4 }

The Trauma That Keeps On Giving And Giving

When I was fifteen, I received a brand spanking new car, a 1979 Monte Carlo. I was getting a new car every six months; if I wasn't blowing a motor, I was running into something. I was the only child in Marionville, especially at the high school, driving a brand new car or one of the very few driving a car at all. The fact that I could even drive at all should have been questioned. I was allowed to drive at the ripe old age of fourteen! I managed this feat because my daddy, as I had stated before, was powerful in Marionville. He was best friends with the county lawman, Sheriff Melvin Linwood. Sheriff Linwood was sort of like an Andy Taylor kind of small-town sheriff. Although, Andy would have arrested me for sure, if I had been driving my fourteen year old black ass around Mayberry.

Of course, this was not my first car. The first was the El-Camino that I had received the previous year. The El Camino was sharp as a tack until daddy started using it every day to feed the cows that we owned. As a gift and a substitute for the battle worn El Camino, daddy bought the Monte Carlo. My classmates would scratch it up with pens and nails out of pure spite and jealousy. Because of this, I only had a couple of friends. They were Sherry, who alerted me about the Stanfordson's girls ambush, and Eldrin. Eldrin was my best friend.

I started going out platonically and hanging out with Eldrin more and more during that year. We were best buddies, partners who were more like a brother and sister than anything. I loved my best friend and he loved me. It was clear to me, at least, that it was a friendship-based relationship, although I don't know how Eldrin viewed it. He knew that I liked the girls, so that part of the equation was not a factor in our friendship.

Eldrin and I would hang out during the week at a dance club over in Jasper, Alabama. At the club, I danced for hours. The entire club patrons would just stand back and watch. I loved to dance. I had aspirations of being a professional dancer at some point in the future. At the time, I could remember always seeing this guy who was not attractive at all. He was small in build and had cross-eyes. He would always ask me for a dance. I would always say no. The night before, I had a vision of Grandma Lenora. She was shaking her head at me as if she was telling me no or not to do something. I screamed and mama came into the room. I told her of my vision. Mama said that it was a sign from her. There was something that I shouldn't do or she was warning me about something that may happen in the near future. If only I had paid closer attention, I could have avoided the catastrophe that was to occur the next day.

The only person I danced with at the club was Eldrin. The night after my vision, Eldrin didn't want to go to the club. He had started dating some girl and he was spending a lot of time with her on the phone. So, I went by myself. While I was on my way to my car after leaving the club for the night, the guy who I kept rejecting was waiting on me in the parking lot. The parking lot was dark.

He flashed a knife and said, "Get in the damn car!"

I got into the back seat. He began to drive but he was having a hard time. It was obvious that he couldn't drive.

"Bitch, I'm going to kill you. Your mother and father will never see you again," he said, in those exact cryptically chilling words.

He took me down a dusky road that was not far from the club. It was an endless path that seemingly led to nowhere.

He held the knife to my throat and shouted, "TAKE OFF YOUR CLOTHES!"

He then held my head down forcefully. I tried to fight, but he was much stronger than me. He raped me repeatedly and relentlessly. After hours of being raped and tortured, he dragged me out of the car and over to a barbed wire fence. He then pushed my head through it. I was bleeding so much that my face looked like a crimson dam overflowing. My vision was blurred by the blood. I was close to losing consciousness. He hit me so hard in the mouth with his fist that I just knew that all my teeth had been knocked out. I couldn't feel them or anything else for that matter, because my face, mouth, and body were numb. Finally, I began talking to him through my bloodied, mussed lips, trying to appear as though I was going along with the assault.

I pleaded, "Let's just go to your place."

Even though I looked like I needed to be in a hospital emergency ward, I did this to try and survive. He told me that he was going to take me to his house, tie me up, and rape me until he decided to kill me. So, after convincing him to go to his place, we left the crime scene. I knew he couldn't drive and that was part of my escape plan. He started driving as badly and erratically as I had predicted. I knew the area well since I drove there to dance practically every week. I mentally planned my jump from the car as he swerved left and right, crossing the dividing line of the road. I'll make my escape at the curve, I told myself.

When he turned the sharp curve going around thirty miles an hour, I reached my hand from the back seat and slowly pushed the seat up. I opened the door quickly and jumped. As soon as I jumped forward he caught my blouse. I was dragged by my ripped blouse alongside the car. Thank God for a couple who was standing near the curb kissing after a date, as the man dropped his lady friend off for the night. I ran to them after the rapist finally stopped the car. He still had to put the car into park before he could come after me. I got up with all my strength and ran like hell.

"Help me! Help me! Please help me!"

The rapist came running. He said to me, "Come on, baby." Then, he said to the couple, "She's just tripping off drugs."

They could put the pieces together as they looked at my face and neck and saw the blood, even though it was dark. They saw that my clothes were ripped and my bloodied face was in a horrible condition.

The guy said, "Go on, sir. We are going to take her inside!"

The couple was white and the man was tall, over six feet in height, much taller than the rapist who was about 5'4.

They called the police. Once the police came, I was first taken to the hospital. After I had given the officers a description, they came to the hospital and said that they had a man in custody. By that time, my parents had made it to the hospital. Daddy was looking at me with an expression of concern although he remained quiet and solemn. The police said they had gone by the club and the man I described was still there, so they brought him in. I had to view a line-up to identify the rapist. We left the hospital and went to the police station and I identified that rabid dog.

My mother told me not to mention the rape to anybody in Marionville if I was asked. Predictably, I was asked about it. There were rumors all over the school as well as the town. Mama worked on the scratches and the bruises that were all over me until I was presentable. In spite of the great treatment that I received from her, I didn't go to school for a week. I denied that the incident had even happened each and every time someone asked. My horrible-looking physical education teacher, who reminded me of the cartoon character Magilla Gorilla, kept looking at me with a smirk and smug look. I knew that she hated me.

Before all this had happened she said to me, "I don't like you because you're just a spoiled brat."

My mother met with that black bitch and she told my mother the same thing that she had said to me; she didn't bite her tongue.

My mother said to me, "Come on, baby, the Lord will take care of her."

I heard, years later, that the guy she ended up marrying became hooked on heavy drugs. Apparently, he eventually stole everything out of their home and sold practically everything that she owned to support his habit. She caught pure hell. I felt that she had brought every bit of it on herself. Karma eventually exacts its justice on everyone. I was not immune to the laws of the universe. However, at that time I didn't know that Karma existed, but eventually I would.

That sick animal of a rapist was put in jail and we had to go to trial in Jasper, Alabama. As a coping mechanism, I tried to pretend as though the rape didn't happen. I guess that sentiment showed on my face during my testimony. As I look back, I can see why the judge gave him only two years after the jury found him guilty. I didn't cry at the time of the verdict. Now I cry all the time whenever I think of him, what he did, and how he got off nearly scott-free, even though he was guilty as hell. He did only seven months of a two year sentence. He was let go because of good behavior.

I was in the same club, less than a year after the assault, when I saw that piece of shit standing on the sidelines of the club. He looked as hideous as he had before. I lost it. I grabbed someone's champagne bottle and smashed it on that dog's head. He turned around and looked at me as if nothing had happened. By that time, the owner and what seemed like every other man in the club grabbed me in order to prevent me from trying to kill that bastard with the bottle. It was good for his safety that the owner put his ass out of the club. In reality, the owner shouldn't have let me into the club in the first place because of my age, despite the fact that I never touched any alcohol. Back in 1979, I guess my parents weren't thinking about a lawsuit. They could very well have sued him. I sat my ass down after that incident. I never went back to that club or any other club for years. I stopped dancing. I shifted my focus to girls, girls, and more girls!

I had it all, but that still wasn't enough for me, at that time. I would always want more. When I was around eighteen years old, I perpetrated a scam for money from my father. I would go to the grocery store to buy groceries with a blank check that daddy had pre-signed. I would always get some money for myself out of it. Ten or twenty dollars a pop was where the pilfering began. Unfortunately, that pittance was not enough for me. I got greedy and I would go into his office while mother was still in there paying the workers on Fridays. I would sneak about three or four checks out of his checkbook. My twisted and self-centered rationale was that daddy had so much money that he wouldn't miss what I took.

Daddy couldn't read, but he could sign his name and count. He couldn't comprehend a single word. So in the evening, I would spend about an hour looking at his signature, until I perfected it. I would sign another blank check. Some days, I would cash it for one hundred dollars or on some Saturdays, when I bought groceries, I would write the check out for fifty dollars more than the price of the bill and get the cash back. I never thought that someone at the cash register may, in all likelihood, have been fucking my daddy. I never thought that anyone would go back and tell him. After about three months of my larceny, one of his whores did, in fact, tell. Daddy came home and questioned me about it. I waffled and evaded the truth. He went from inquiry to point blank telling me what I had done. He was mad as hell. I had fucked up everything, my sweet life and my free ride through life.

Daddy picked up a mop stick and broke it in half. I wasn't a fool. I knew what that meant. So, I ran to the back of the house, to my room, and locked the door. Daddy came to the door with that stick and said, "Molly you better open this damn door!"

I did, and he came in and started beating the shit out of me with that half of a mop. I cried so hard that I peed all over myself. It was so horrific that mama was crying, too. Before this check writing incident escalated to the exclamation point of an ass-beating, I had gotten up my nerve and brashly showed mama what I had been doing with daddy's checks.

In a sad voice while shaking her head, she said, "Baby, if daddy finds out, he will kill you. You got to stop this." My hard-headed ass didn't listen to her. Mama tried to remind me about what happened to my brother Blake when he shot my sister Alice in the hand with the BB gun that he got at Christmas. I should have paid attention. Daddy beat Blake with an extension coil to within what seemed an inch of his life. Mama had to nurse him with salve and white cloths because his welts were so severe. Yes, I had fucked up for real this time.

At that time, I had a limited edition 1981 white Trans Am that daddy had bought for me. There were only five thousand made by Pontiac. I had the only one in the state of Alabama. However, daddy wasn't paying any more car notes after my major screw-up. Here I was riding around with my arm in a sling because of that ass beating. I had no more perks. My free ride was fucked all to hell because of my greediness. The Stanfordson family, with whom I still had an ongoing love-hate, but mostly hateful relationship with, loved it. He had told his bitches that he wasn't paying any more car notes for me. Daddy had a gas pump in the yard. Although this was primarily for his work trucks, I had unlimited access to the "free" gas. I had messed that up, too. I was not allowed to get any more gas out of the pump, even if my life had depended on it.

My life has always seemed to take some unexpected twists, although most of them were of my own doing. I just would never have predicted later in life the events that occurred, as they had in my younger years. Looking back at the events many years later, they all seemed so improbable. This is just one example of how my life is part enigma and part contradiction. In this case, less than two years after the check writing incident, my mother bought me another red Corvette. It was a thing of beauty. This was my third corvette. She was able to buy it because she had started her own business processing pulpwood. Sadly, it didn't last because she hired lazy alcoholics who didn't want to work. At the time, "Little Red Corvette" by Prince and the Revolution was number one on the charts. I was the shit again. Of course, I guess I always really felt that way about myself. The Corvette made me "extra shitty."

Here was yet another ironic and paradoxical twist to my convoluted life. I had married Eldrin, who had been more of a partner and my "play brother" as I alluded to earlier. Eldrin wanted to marry me even though he knew of my craving for females. I agreed because I actually did love him, but as a friend loves another friend. Shortly after we were married, Eldrin went off to the army and was to be stationed in Korea. I told him that I wanted to stay in the United States.

I said, "Since you will only be there for one year, you go. I will be here when you get back." He was furious but he reluctantly agreed. We remained married for less than a year, but in that time I was getting a small check for two hundred dollars every month because I was his wife. The two hundred dollars helped on the four hundred a month Corvette car payment. Eldrin wanted me to sell the car but I told him no. Eldrin had two sons by his next door neighbor's daughter and I held that over his head like a sword.

How can you tell me to sell anything, when you won't take care of your two damn sons from your next door neighbor?

That was my answer to that request. Even though my rationalization of using his sons had nothing to do with my defense of not selling my car, that was my stand and I stood by it. Once again, our marriage was a microcosm of my chaotic life. One filled with contradictions and mixed messages.

One, Eldrin knew that I preferred women. Two, even though we were intimate as man and wife, it was more of a perfunctory act than romance. Hell, I made love with Vickie Gregg, my first love, who I kept in touch with, on our wedding night. Three, we married for the most absurd of reason — we loved each other as friends. We didn't ever want to lose that friendship. That reasoning was as flawed then, as it now seems to me today. The marriage caused a rift in our relationship that was irreparable.

Eldrin transformed from buddy to husband instantaneously. I was not having that at all. I was going to accommodate his needs sexually, but I was not going to be ordered around like a passive housewife. The event that signaled the end of our union was that I had driven way out to someplace in the boondocks, maybe a six hour drive, to the military base where Eldrin was leaving from. Chauncey, his brother and I drove all that way to see him before he went to Korea. That drive must have been four hundred miles. It was in Georgia, Fort Benning, I think. Eldrin told me beforehand that he had gotten a hotel for me and Chauncey, plus a pass to the military base. When we got there, we couldn't get on the base because his dumb ass didn't arrange for the base pass. To compound that nonsense, I was hungry as hell. I hadn't had a thing to eat since the morning of our trip.

Chauncey had the bright idea to put on Eldrin's military jacket, which we had brought with us to give to Eldrin, since he left it at our home in Marionville. He used it to go into the mess hall for food. Chauncey asked the servers to give him one more piece of chicken. He gave that one piece to me by sneaking it out of the mess hall in a napkin. Eldrin didn't even offer to get me any food after we finally caught up with him. That one chicken breast barely kept my hunger at bay, nor did he act as if he cared one bit. After that bullshit treatment, I'd had enough of being Eldrin's wife and friend. I hurried up and took my hungry ass back to mama and Marionville. It was a shame that we had to go our separate ways. We had been through a lot of good and bad times, but there was no doubt that we were ending on a down note. Eldrin and I were divorced near the end of 1982.

Once Eldrin went off to Korea, his sister Sophie started calling me every day asking me to come to get her and take her riding. It didn't take long to discover that this was a ruse. She really wanted to have sex with me. We did. However, it was more sexual contact, such as kissing, fondling of breasts, and hunching. Yes, this was my still-husband's sister! I was cheating on Eldrin with yet another woman and this one was in his immediate family. It was just wrong and as I look back on it, many years later, I can truthfully admit as much. Even though I didn't approach Sophie with any desires I had for her, I didn't decline the invitation. What was wrong with me that I could even entertain the thought? It was as if I had this hate or some sort of unresolved issue in me. Sex was the way that I had tried to resolve that hostility. Many times, people who were sexually abused acted out sexually. I had not been abused in any way except for the sexual assault at the dance club. I can only hope that I can find an answer to this perplexing part of my psyche.

I can remember back to the time before all of this, when we were no more than buddies and Eldrin discussed with me the fact that he was fucking this girl, Alinda, when he was fifteen years old. He got her pregnant and then he went back and got her pregnant again a year later at age sixteen. I could not believe Eldrin had gotten her pregnant, not once but twice based on what he used to say about her. Eldrin would call her a gorilla and the two children little gorillas.

He would always say, "Those are not my kids. I wouldn't touch that damn monkey!"

That girl was not attractive at all. She also had a speech impediment. He totally had me believing him for the longest time. I couldn't imagine him fucking that gorilla ass, but, to be frank, I didn't give a shit. We were partners and I had women on my brain.

****

Woo was silent, with a pregnant pause, before she spoke.

"Now, wait a damn minute! You had your daddy just about giving you the world and you fucked that up by stealing chump change. He beat your ass with a mop. You seduced a fourteen year old girl. And this rape! How in the world did you not tell me about this during the eight years that I have known you? Bitch, I can't believe your ass! How in the hell did you go from being friends with Eldrin to marrying him and then fucking with his sister?"

"I don't know, girl. Like I said, we wanted to keep the friendship. So we married. His sister came on to me," I sighed.

"Shit, girl. The way that you keep the friendship is by sending Hallmark cards, calling the mutherfucker on his birthday or taking his ass out to a club or for dinner from time to time, not getting married. Molly, you're a fucking trip for real!" Woo laughed out loud.

She was laughing so hard that you could hear her literally crying over the telephone.

"Hey, I can't explain it. I was young and stupid, I guess. Hell, I don't know, that was like twenty years ago. Ain't you ever made a mistake, Ho?" I said, laughing because Woo's laughter was so infectious.

"Damn, girl. Mistake is your middle name and your last name is I make bad," Woo joked.

"Okay, there's more. I haven't gotten to the halfway point. You tired?" I asked. I had been talking for 'bout four hours and the time had blown by.

"This shit is real. I'm wide awake. So, get to talking."

****

{ CHAPTER 5 }

I Must Be A Magnet For Trouble

After my short-lived marriage to Eldrin, I decided to have mama to go ahead and trade the Corvette and get something a little cheaper. So, we got a 1981 Nissan 280 ZX. I drove it back and forth to my job in Greenville, Alabama. I worked part-time for my mother's doctor, Jesse J. Howard. My mother didn't trust any doctors in Marionville, so she went to Dr. Howard, who was a black man. I was working from 4 to 8 PM Monday through Friday. I made about a hundred dollars per week and cleared eighty dollars after I paid for gas. I learned a lot working for Dr. Howard. The most important thing I learned was how to administer injections.

This was a blessing because three months later I had to stop working for him. Mama found out that she was a diabetic and her blood sugar was over four hundred. She had to start taking insulin immediately. I would give her an injection in the morning and one in the afternoon until she learned how to do it herself. Dr. Howard never tried to come on to me while I worked for him. He was very professional. His professionalism really struck me. If you are going to be about your business, do so and keep your business and personal life separate. It was a rule that I adhered to from that point forward, at least as best as I could given my personality. As I had learned, nothing was ever as good or as bad as it seemed. Up to that point, things were never quite that good.

This was the time that I had made the semi-permanent move to West Palm Beach. It was after my failed marriage to Eldrin. The situation with my parents was temporary. I had to make a move in order to press forward in my life. I met two so-called religious "prophets" shortly after my arrival in West Palm. I had gone to them for some good luck. I became intimately involved with the first prophet in 1983. This religious swindler was a white man who had the biggest dick I had seen in my life! I became pregnant by him because he told me that he couldn't have any kids. I allowed him to have unprotected sex with me without a condom.

Surprisingly, I never used any type of birth control. I had been amazingly lucky with my other interactions with men as to not have gotten pregnant. I became involved with the second prophet three years later. He had a brand new white Rolls Royce, which seemed to be a perk of his being such a shyster. He had the first cellular phone that I had ever seen. He would flaunt his cell phone by talking with people while we were out at restaurants. It was probably costing him a dollar a minute. He was "all that and a bag of chips" in my opinion. He was husband and father material in my mind, but I wasn't ready to have anybody's child. Even with this fact firmly in my mind, I somehow became pregnant by this prophet, also. In both cases, I was young and gullible. I was seduced by their words and financial trappings. Those things mattered a lot. If you didn't have money, you could just forget about Molly.

I cannot fully explain why I was sleeping with men, marrying them, and still craving women. Maybe, I was just being an opportunistic. At that time, the term 'gold digger' did not exist. I don't even know that the term would be accurate. I did take advantage of the fact that men wanted to spend their time and money on me.

Around this time, I applied for a job with the post office. I received a letter from the postal service stating that I passed the test and that I could start employment in sixty days. The problem was that the postal service was not hiring pregnant women and I was. The father was none other than the second prophet.

This was my second abortion. I went back to Alabama for both abortions. There was yet another unbelievable assault on me during the second abortion. Both abortions were performed by the "professional" Dr. Howard. During the second procedure, I woke up prematurely from the anesthetic to find Dr. Howard on top of me having sex. I was so out of it that I only remember him saying 'it won't take long.' When I left his office, I couldn't say anything, not one single, solitary word. Eventually, I told mama what Dr. Howard had done. She said for me to just try to forget about it. I tried. Nine years later, I could still feel the mental after-effects of the assault. I called the Alabama Medical Board because I was having problems dealing with the trauma of it all.

The medical board informed me that Dr. Howard's license had been revoked for five years. He couldn't practice medicine anymore. I asked them why, but they wouldn't go into any of the details. In reality, I already knew why based upon the unethical and criminal act he had performed on me. I couldn't understand why he didn't try to date me while I was working for him. Why did he have to wait until I was lying defenseless on an operating table to make his move? The only conclusion I could come to was that he was a rapist hiding behind the well respected and trusted white coat of a physician. I live with the regret each day that I didn't report him. I wish that I never had either of those abortions. I ask God for His forgiveness for those acts all of the time. I'm just not sure if He has accepted my apology.

"Do you think he did anything to you the first time?" Woo inquired.

I paused for a moment before I answered.

"I don't know," I responded.

I got married again. This time it was to a white man that I met in West Palm Beach. It was a short-lived union. We were only married for three months. His name was Josh T. Martin. He was much older, about fourteen years my senior. Of course, he was not hurting financially. I was such a lady and perfect wife to Josh. Everything was perfect until he told me that my nieces couldn't come over to his house to visit me anymore.

"Why?" I questioned.

"Because they are too dark," he responded.

I cursed that bastard out "Aunt Rocksie style." I used words that I am sure no one had ever heard before. Maybe I should have taken more time to have gotten to know Josh properly. I would have learned that he was a racist bigot who wanted his thrill of being with black women. He had probably dated black females before; yet, he had a "plantation mentality" about black women. Apparently, the dark ones were only good enough to serve the 'masser' or for the 'masser' to fuck in secret to make mulatto babies. To be a "house nigger," you had to be light-skinned. It was no major loss. He was as terrible a lover as I had ever known. His two-minute-a-day sex was horrible.

During our brief marriage, Josh would put me out of the house all the time, especially when he wanted to be with his women. Despite this fact, I remained faithful right up until the very end of our relationship. I even considered him to be a nice looking man until I found false teeth and a fake hairpiece in the bathroom. As I look back on it, Josh putting me out of his house wasn't that bad of a deal.

I didn't love Josh Martin at all. I married him because I was tired of Aunt Lula Bell, the relative I stayed with until I established myself in West Palm. She turned off the hot water in her house in the winter time to save money. There was no ventilation in the house at all. In the room, where I slept, the windows were sealed. It was always hot as hell in her house. I paid the utility bills out of the same money that a friend had given me. My mother offered to put an air unit in aunt's house, but aunt said no. My aunt's house was paid for, so she didn't ask me for any rent. It was just too stifling to be in such a closed-in space. I married Josh purely and simply to get out of Aunt Lula Bell's house.

In between evictions by my soon-to-be ex-husband, I met Andrew Brewington. He really became infatuated with me. Andrew was seventy-two years of age when I met him. So, he was fifty years older than me. He was about five foot seven and slender. He always had a cigar dangling from the side of his mouth, whether lit or not. It was Andrew Brewington's green Rolls that I drove back and forth to Marionville during my weekend trysts with Sonya Stanfordson. He couldn't have sex because of some medical problems. His love of alcohol didn't help matters, yet he had many lady friends.

It was pretty clear that the women who were coming by to visit him were doing so just to get money. He loved it. Strangely enough, I really cared for him, even though he served no useful purpose other than to provide shelter for me when Josh inevitably threw me out. After a while, he even stopped giving me money, but I still wanted to be with him. He was so much fun. He had the spirit of a twenty year old. It was perfect, no sex, just companionship. After my divorce from Josh Martin, I tried to get Andrew to marry me, but he wouldn't.

Andrew told my mother that he wanted her to come down to West Palm from Marionville. He was going to quick claim one of his rental properties to me and so she did. We were all sitting in the lawyer's conference room. The lawyer put the papers in front of Andrew Brewington and, for some reason that only he knew, he wouldn't sign the documents. My mother had come all the way to West Palm at his request only to see him change his mind. I was mad as hell. It was at that point that I decided to let go of Andrew Brewington for good.

Being the human paradox that I am, I truly believed that I loved Andrew and that I would have been so good for him and to him. Why I had this passion and affinity for him, I cannot tell you, but I really did. Maybe, it had something to do with the regret that I had for not spending any appreciable time with my Granddaddy Jake. Perhaps, Andrew was substituting for some sort of grandfather void that I had. Maybe my love for him was confused in my addled mind. Instead of the boyfriend-girlfriend type, it was simply the same as what you would feel for a favorite uncle.

I often think of him to this day, years after his passing. During this time, I had begun working at the postal service. He had a great deal of influence in that. He died within the three months of my probationary period with the West Palm Post Office. I didn't know that he had died until one of his friends came by Aunt Lula Bell's home.

I had gone by aunt's to get some sleep because I couldn't get any at the condo I had just purchased. My neighbor's ten year old bad ass boy, Jeremy, was always climbing on top of my roof intentionally to awake me. I finally called DFACS and that put a stop to him.

"You called DFACS on somebody's child? Woo asked.

I responded, " I didn't want to, but his mother wouldn't do anything with his bad ass. I had to get some sleep. Hell, I was working the grave-yard shift and that little bastard knew it. He would do shit deliberately to wake me up. I will never forget that Little Green-Eyed Fucker!"

"Damn, Molly. So, what ever happened when the man came by your aunt's?"

The man said, "I see that you are doing ok."

I asked him, "What do you mean?"

He said, "You don't know."

"Know what?"

Andrew had died and they had already had his funeral. I called his sister right away. She said that she tried to get in contact with me, but she didn't have any numbers for me nor did she know where my aunt lived. I was so hurt. I said to myself, I know that God meant for it to happen this way. I was under my probationary period and I couldn't miss work. If I had known, I would have been so depressed. I probably would have called in sick for sure.

Andrew had helped me get the job with the postal service with his personal contacts, but more specifically through his drinking associate who was in management at the postal service. In the afternoons after he left work, he would go to the Sunset Lounge, his favorite watering hole. He always wanted me to meet him there.

He was usually full of alcohol, but he would always ask this one particular man, who always seemed to be at the Lounge, "Help my baby get on with the post office." Finally, one day, the man said to me, "I want you to come down to my office tomorrow." Hell, I didn't really want to work, but Andrew Brewington made it a point to get my ass up out of the bed whenever he got up for work. This day was no exception.

I went to the post office to see this man whose name I can't remember. He told me to sign up for the test. I took the test and, within a month, found out I had passed with a high grade. This must have been Andrew's purpose in my life. Everyone we meet is put in our path for some reason, be it good or bad. After Andrew passed away, his sister allowed the Rolls Royce to sit and rust away. She could have given it to me, instead. I had the car all of the time when Andrew was alive. She never drove it at all. It literally sat and rotted into a pile of green and rusted red steel.

Around 1985, when I was again living with my Aunt Lula Bell, Andrew and I were on bad terms and he had kicked me out of the house. I heard about this young dentist who was black and single. I had two gold teeth in the front of my mouth that I badly wanted removed. They didn't look bad. However, I have to admit that the gold teeth did make me look country as hell. I could tell that it was hindering me from getting a good job. Because of this, I made it my business to set up an appointment with this dentist to get my teeth taken care of.

I also had a few missing teeth in the back of my mouth that needed to be replaced.

"Why you had missing teeth?" Woo asked.

I replied, "Well, the dentist that we had when I was growing up in Marionville was nothing but a damn drunk. Every time someone had a toothache; he would simply pull the tooth. He was such a bumpkin of a dentist that he didn't know anything about root canals or any other method of preserving teeth."

I arrived for my appointment. The assistant put me in a room. Eventually, the doctor came in.

"Hi, how are you?" he asked, and for some reason he looked a little nervous.

"I'm doing just fine, except for my teeth," I joked. I was a little nervous too.

"Well, what made you decide to get the gold for your teeth?"

"I was young and my mom and dad have gold teeth, so it seemed like the thing to do. I really don't like them at all," I said

"I'm going to set you up for an appointment to come back in a couple of weeks. I will see what I can do to change that," he said.

"I don't have any insurance," I sighed.

"We're not going to worry about that right now. We're going to go ahead today and clean your teeth. This will be on me. Just make sure that you leave your contact information with the young lady out front," he said.

I said okay to him while giving him my sexiest, most coquettish look. All the while that I was talking to him he was grinning like a Cheshire cat. His name was Jack. He was the complete visual definition of a nerd, at least as far as black nerds are concerned. Dr. Jack's hair was kinky and it looked as though it had never been combed. I had never in my life seen a person with such bad hair. However, he was neither ugly nor handsome. He had a nice body to go with a beautiful smile. Everything appeared to be falling into place; Dr. Jack called me the same night at my aunt's house.

"Hello, Molly. Did I catch you at a bad time?" he asked.

I was still a little nervous. "No, I'm not doing anything. Why do you ask?"

"I was wondering if you would like to come over to my place." he said.

"Well, it's late and I don't feel like driving."

"Where do you live? I can come over and pick you up," Dr. Jack said.

I agreed to see him since he was picking up the tab for a lot of dental work. It was worth a little bit of my time. So, I had no problem accepting the invitation. I knew that the trade-off was sex for services rendered. I was more than willing to fulfill my end of the bargain. Dr. Jack took me over to his apartment. In a short time, we were getting down to business. Lovemaking was quick and horrible! It was terrible. Sex, however, was a necessary evil. I needed to have my teeth fixed. Interestingly, he had never experienced a blow job. So, it was a tremendous experience for him to have me go down on him. If I had known that Dr. Jack was that much of a greenhorn, as it pertained to lovemaking, I could have taken his ass for a ride, if I had chosen to. However, I needed the dental work badly. Using him for anymore than what I needed was more energy than I was willing to expend at the time.

We remained friends even after I moved to Valletta. The relationship eventually became one of my supplying the medication to soothe the ache of his sweet tooth for females. On every occasion he arrived in Georgia I procured a beautiful slim woman with long hair to accompany him for the weekend. After a few years, he had gotten up the nerve and confidence to stay in contact with the tricks. So, he graduated to setting up his own sex appointments. Nowadays, I don't even hear a word from his black ass.

"When was the last time that you heard from ol' Jack?" Woo asked.

"Girl, it's been a while now, like a year and a half or more. The last thing I heard was that he was involved with one of those hook-ups. You know Avalon? She's that fine ass redbone."

"Yeah, I know Avalon. She's pretty. I can't imagine Dr. Jack and her together as a couple, though," Woo replied.

"I think that they're just sex partners. Guess what?"

"What?"

"Dr. Jack told me that Avalon let him fuck her straight up the ass!" I said.

"Aw Naw, girl. You are lying! I think that any man who will fuck a woman in the ass will fuck a man if he got enough alcohol in him," Woo joked.

"Hell, yeah! He will. An asshole is an asshole. You don't see no face. Just plain ol' ass!" I said.

We both laughed so hard at this statement that I nearly peed on myself.

As I think back to that era in my life, I would be remiss not to mention Gino Halliburton, even if he is nothing more than a footnote. Before Josh, Andrew, or the prophets, I was trying on West Palm for size. I was just visiting to see if I wanted to make it a semi-permanent home, at least as far as my nomadic lifestyle would permit at the time. I met Gino and he instantly fell in love with me. I wasn't sure if I was going to stay in West Palm at the time or not. As I said, I was visiting. I still had the red Corvette, so I was post-Eldrin, but just by a few months. Gino's parents had plenty of money. He wanted to get an apartment for me and move me to West Palm. I tried to see where this offer would lead. We had an intimate relationship, but I hated the sex. We only had sex once a week. It was all for his benefit, obviously. He complained about it, but I stuck to my guns. I just couldn't deal with his ugly black ass. He had a big ass dick, which was too much, considering that I was not that attracted to him. Maybe it could be said that I took advantage of the situation. Gino approached me with the proposal. I was not in a position financially, at that time in my life, to have been too selective.

One Friday night, when Gino came home, something was in the air. I knew something was going to happen or that I was going to instigate whatever it was that was to happen. It turned out to be the latter. At around nine o'clock, I asked Gino for the four hundred dollars. I needed to send it home to my mother to pay my car note. He told me that I had to wait a while because he didn't have it right then. I yelled these three words before I knew that I had said them: YOU BLACK MUTHERFUCKER! That nigger slapped me so damn hard that I saw stars for real. I knew that he hated that he had hit me. But by that time, there was no turning back. Gino was so mad that he couldn't speak to me. So, he just left the apartment. As soon as his ass hit the pavement, I packed the few clothes that I had with me and put them behind the seat of the Corvette. I headed back to Marionville. By twelve in the morning, I was on the turnpike headed north. He called and called and begged me to come back. He asked my mother if she would speak with me. My mother had met Gino and his entire family and, though she had an opinion, she decided to remain neutral. She told me that it was up to me.

I said, "Mama, I am not going back. He hit me and that was that."

I later heard that he married the same girl he had his child with. That was really where my four dollars went on that Friday night. Hell, he might have thought so, but I wasn't stupid by a long shot.

****

"Ummm, Uh! Girl! You got pregnant by two fake ass prophets. You were raped in your sleep by a doctor who was giving you an abortion from the fake ass prophets. You married a white man who hated dark black women. You were in love with a seventy-two year old man who was old enough to be your granddaddy. You fucked a man who disgusted you just to keep an apartment. Girl, you were one messed up heifer back then! No wonder your ass is so crazy!" Woo laughed.

I started laughing before I could speak. "Shut the hell up! You're crazy, too!" I said between the laughter.

"Ok, you can go on. Now that I've gotten my laugh on," Woo said.

"This is more than you ever thought you would ever hear about me, huh?"

"Your life is some of the craziest shit that I've ever heard, Molly."

"There's more, girl. A lot more. With me, it seemed that there always was," I said.

In order to better understand who I am now, I have had to continually re-examine my past and the people who influenced me.

{ CHAPTER 6 }

The Curse That Keeps Me Cursing

I became acquainted with Willie Mae four months after my relationship with Eldrin was over. At this time, she was a big time drug dealer from Mobile, Alabama. She came to Marionville a few times a month for "business" and to see me. I met Willie Mae at the local convenience station while I was there filling up the 280ZX, which my mother had traded for the beloved Corvette. Willie Mae pulled up in her big luxury sedan. After I introduced myself, we struck up a conversation.

I took her over to my parents' house to meet my mother. I wanted her to know who I was visiting while I was in Mobile. Mama didn't know that Willie Mae was a drug dealer. Even if she had known, she was always nonjudgmental and would have reserved her opinions. Willie Mae was around fifty years of age. She was considerably older than me. She had this big, black Lincoln Continental and a driver. He drove her around the state to pick up her drugs and make her deals just like a rich woman would, or for that matter, a mob boss. She gave me money every time I saw her and that was practically every day for about a month. I even went with her on a couple of drug runs out to New Orleans.

"Hold up. Let me get this clear. Was this BEFORE you moved to Palm Beach?" Woo asked.

"Yup," I said. "Let me take you back in time. I have to tell you this to make a point."

"Excuse me, bitch. Press on," Woo said.

While Willie Mae snorted cocaine, I sat in the middle seat of the car, with my young, stupid ass, oblivious to how dangerous this woman could be. I never told my mother about Willie Mae's personal life and she never asked one question. I would just tell her that I was driving down to Mobile and that I would be back later on in the evening. That was as forthright as I would be with her at the time. Willie Mae had a huge home with lots of people coming and going all of the damn time. She wanted me there with her all of the time. She was snorting this drug called "skag," otherwise known as heroin. She seemed to enjoy being high all of the time, so I decided to try it just to see what the big deal was. I figured that since she did it, and since people paid her for the drug, it must have been something else. What in the hell did I do that for?

After I snorted a little of the skag, I became paralyzed from the top of my head down to the tips of my toes. The only things that I could move were my eyes. I laid on Wille Mae's couch for two hours. I could hear everybody walking by me as they came into her house asking Willie Mae and her henchmen,

"What in the hell is wrong with her?" They, meaning Willie Mae and her accomplices, would say to the customers, "She'll be ok. Come on in. So, what do you need?" I was so scared because I was lying there incapacitated for what seemed like days. More than two hours had elapsed before the paralysis was finally over. After that incident I left Willie Mae's house and I never called her again, never answered her calls, and never went back to her house.

Later in the year, as I watched the nightly news at my mother's home, lo and behold, there was Willie Mae and her cronies being busted for drugs. They were being herded into police cars. I heard that she received federal prison time. As I think back on that time, if I had continued on my path of association with Willie Mae, I might have been serving time, also. As I look back on that time in my life, I was either attracting negative people toward me or, at the very least, constantly putting myself in precarious situations.

Many years before Willie Mae, when I was about fifteen, I met a lady by the name of Nicole. She was at least thirty years of age at that time. She was very attractive with a nice beautiful smile, a nice figure, nice brown skin, and nice golden hair. She drove a sporty car with T- tops. She kept a big bankroll of money and would always flash it in front of me. She would always have at least two thousand dollars on her every time I saw her. The allures of maturity and money was intoxicating to my young, materialistic mind. Now that I think about it. Those two factors have been the common denominators in many of my relationships with men and women. I fell in love with Nicole. I knew that she had plenty of money, but I had no idea how she came about those finances. Since she never seemed to do anything but spend, spend, and spend some more. I would imagine that maybe she was a model, actress, or, even to the seedier side, a stripper or prostitute. I never asked her for any money, but she would always give it to me. Nothing really came of my infatuation, at that point in time, but we kept in touch. It became clear, as time went on, that the feeling was mutual.

Years later, in 1982, one year after I graduated from high school, Nicole and I rekindled our friendship. I ended up moving out to New Orleans to live with her. I came home every other week with Nicole whenever she came to visit her family. I ended up living with her for six months.

Eventually, things started going really badly for Nicole. She became heavily involved with drugs, which eroded her finances. By that time, I had discovered that the money that Nicole was flaunting was a windfall settlement from an injury her husband suffered while working on an oil rig. They had been living high and mighty on borrowed time. The money was not enough to support their lifestyle forever. Around the fourth month, she told me that our arrangement was only temporary. She said that if I needed to live somewhere permanently, I needed to move in with Beni, her dope friend. She said I could get money from Beni to pay my car note every month. So, I did just that. It was either get a job or use that alternative. Those were my only two choices at that moment. I found "The Beni Option" to be the best choice. I had to fuck his old ugly ass almost every other night. It was awful, just horrible. I hated each and every minute of it.

Nicole's husband, Morgan, was a spineless jellyfish. She treated him as though he was a child. She screamed at him constantly and he acted just like a little puppy. He knew I was sleeping in bed every night with Nicole when I lived with them. I heard that Morgan was injured pretty badly on that oil rig where he worked. Allegedly, he couldn't have sex.

This was what Beni said, so I don't know if this information was fact or hearsay. I believed that Beni was fucking Nicole as well. He did everything she told him to. He paid my car note for about two months. The experience was so revolting. I couldn't deal with him or Nicole anymore. I left them both and I went back to Marionville. I believed Nicole eventually became jealous of Beni giving me the money that she could have been getting from him. Her drug problem had gotten progressively worse. It went from marijuana to powder cocaine, and eventually to crack.

During the time that I was in New Orleans, I met this guy named Steffen at a gas station. He instantly fell head over heels in love with me. We would talk on the phone for hours while I was in New Orleans. We even continued conversing after I moved back to Alabama. I started visiting him at his home in Port Sulfur, Louisiana. It was an hour and a half from New Orleans. I didn't mind the long trips or the conversations because I genuinely liked Steffen.

Steffen never pressured me into having sex, and I never broached the subject. So, we never did. Incredibly, he gave me five thousand dollars for no reason other than that he liked me. I hung on to that money from 1983 up until 1987 when I started working for the postal service. During my ninety day probationary period, I used the five thousand dollars as a down payment on the condo that I couldn't rest in because of my neighbor's little bad ass green-eyed boy.

Steffen sent me two hundred dollars every month from the very first month that I met him. He didn't stop sending me money for nearly twenty years. The reason that he stopped was that he became hooked on crack cocaine really badly. He also started fucking prostitutes. Both vices would take a large chunk out of anyone's bank account. We remained friends for years. I comforted him via the phone, when his dad and brother passed away, and whenever he needed moral support. I tried to persuade Steffen to move to West Palm, but he didn't want to. He visited me a couple of times, but there was never any sex involved.

The last real contact that I had with Steffen was when I spoke to him right before Hurricane Katrina devastated the state of Louisiana in 2005. I have written him letters and they all were returned as undeliverable. I have tried to find him over the internet, but I couldn't find any information concerning him or his family. I am too afraid to contact the Red Cross because they might tell me that both he and his family are dead. This would hurt me. I loved Steffen in my own special way. I cared for his family and I often think about him, his mother Margaret, and his sister Jenny. I hope he and his family are alive and doing well. If they are, I wonder if Steffen ever thinks about me. One day, I am going to get up enough nerve to call the Red Cross. I wasn't in love with Steffen, but I cared for him and loved him as a friend. I told him as much, yet he still wanted to marry me badly. He knew what he wanted and it was me. It was just too bad that the feeling was not mutual.

As the years passed, I so desperately wanted to get closer to my mother. In 1991, I finally received a transfer from the West Palm Post Office to the South Georgia branch.

It wasn't very long afterwards that I fell in love with a sophisticated, worldly woman named Paula. She was twenty two years older than me. She was also the manager at my job, which lends to both the dicey nature of our relationship, as well as its intrigue. After I was intimate with Paula, I vowed to never be with another man, but that vow didn't last long. To this day, I believe now more than ever that she was the one woman who truly convinced me of my affinity for women. Paula had class, style, and grace. To describe the ideal woman for me, she had it all! Paula reminded me of Diana Ross, minus the long haired wig and big eyes.

We were together for a total of eight years. After I met Paula, no love I had for any woman in my life, either past or present, could compare to the love that I had for her. However, things changed after the sixth year. Prior to that time, we were very happy, but it was at that point that sex between us stopped completely and we began to fight. The so-called love making for six years didn't involve oral sex.

"You guys never had oral sex?" Woo asked.

"Naw — she didn't like oral sex at all," I said slowly and ashamed.

"What the hell did you do?"

"Use the Dildo. It kept us both content."

"Ay, girl! She wanted dick, a REAL dick," Woo laughed out loud.

"Shut the hell up, Woo. It lasted for six years."

The fighting accelerated from being just verbal to actual physical abuse on my part. I even put a gun to her head once. I threatened to kill her if she left me. That threat kept her with me for another two horrible years. She finally left me in 1998 for some other women's husband. To add insult to injury, I caught them together. I was so emotionally devastated that it took years before I was able to get myself together again.

"Hell, you should have known that shit wasn't gonna last! Molly, you're crazy for real!" Woo said laughing.

I said, "If I could say one thing to her right now, it would be that she didn't deserve the treatment I gave her. I am SO sorry. Of course, that apology would probably fall on deaf ears."

"Molly, I don't blame Paula for leaving your ass. Hell, you

beat that lady. I can't believe that she took that shit from your tiny little ass," Woo said pointedly.

"I don't know why I was doing that in the first place. Maybe, if Paula had just fought back, I might have stopped. That just goes to show, you don't have to be a man to abuse a woman," I sighed.

"How could you beat up Paula, who was taller and bigger than you, but not fight off a rapist who was closer to your size?" Woo asked.

"There's a big difference between being mad and being scared. It was like I had extra strength or something when I was pissed off at Paula. Hell, I don't know. Just let me get back to this story because it's getting late," I said.

I started to question whether or not things were ever going to go my way in terms of finding love. Paula was involved with a married man. The fact that I had caught them together was concrete visual evidence. It was a hard thing to stomach, but it was the truth. She cheated on me and there was no turning back. I loved Paula more than I had any other woman. Apparently, my love was not good enough for her.

"You mean your FAKE DICK wasn't good enough," Woo chuckled.

"Whatever."

In my self-directed mind, I thought that I had given her all of the love that she needed, but the fact that she had to find love in the arms of someone other than me was the crushing blow of reality. I can't say that I am not somewhat to blame for my failed relationship with Paula. I abused her verbally and physically. How do I justify hurting the one woman I professed to love more than any other? Once again, I must admit that I was sometimes guilty of creating my own despair.

A few months after Paula and I broke up, Sherry, my friend

who had alerted me to the Stanfordson sisters' ambush after school and who had been my friend since the first grade, confessed to me that she'd had an affair with a woman. Sherry knew about my relationships with women. She had, however, never hinted that she had any such inclinations. Surprisingly, Sherry suggested that we get together. I agreed because I was single and it was just sex. It was horrible because she was so physically unappealing. She had a wide ass, her tits hung down like a cow's udder and she had a gut. Nevertheless, we were intimate three times. The only reason was because any female contact was a balm for my pain over losing Paula. I used Sherry like a person uses a drink of alcohol, to soothe and to forget.

After Sherry, it was female after female with the occasional male thrown in. The men had something that could benefit me. They wanted to give me what I needed in exchange for the opportunity to sleep with me. With men, it was primarily business, but with women it was personal and physical. I still had my old policy active — if you didn't have money, you don't have Molly.

I met a woman, after my debacle with Sherry, named Danielle. She was employed in a profession which paid her well over six figures. She was attractive, to boot. I felt as though I had hit the jackpot with Danielle. She really dug me. After two weeks of dating, we ended up at my place. We couldn't make it to my bed. We were kissing and heatedly tearing off each others' clothes. Right in the midst of this, Danielle abruptly stopped

"Wait, Molly, I have something to tell you," Danielle said with a somber tone of voice.

I was thinking to myself that Danielle would say that she had a boyfriend or even a girlfriend.

"I have herpes," Danielle revealed.

I instantly went from burning hot to ice cold within milliseconds.

"How did it happen, Danielle?" I tried to ask with concern, but as far as I was concerned it was a clinical question that a psychiatrist would ask rather than a potential lover.

"I was raped by an African man who had the disease," Danielle answered. She wasn't making any eye contact.

I became saddened after talking with Danielle for hours because it was a tragic story. However, I knew that there was no future between us. I knew that the inevitable question was coming.

"Is this going to change anything between us?" Danielle asked with a pleading look in her eyes.

I said no, but she could sense that it was not the truth.

"Are you sure?" She asked again with a tone that suggested she was pleading her case rather than seeking reassurance.

"Yes, Danielle," I said and kissed her. "Let's go to sleep."

Danielle and I spent that Saturday and Sunday together until she had to leave, which was that Sunday night. I didn't call her much after that revelation. I didn't answer her calls. One weekend, Danielle came to my door and banged on it for nearly an hour. She eventually took the hint after so many brush-offs that I was no longer interested in being involved with her. Danielle must have been very much in love with me.

I don't know if my experiences with the rapes were the catalysts that began my mental alienation from men. I can only say that I have no real desire for men from a sexual standpoint. In other words, there is no physical "craving" to have a man like there is for me to possess a woman. One thing that is for sure is my life would have been vastly different if I had never been raped. Those traumatic experiences had not changed my desire for women, but they were contributing factors to all the confusion and bad decisions. Without that trauma, I would have had a clearer perspective much younger. The rapes started to fuck with me years later. Only after I sought treatment did I come to grips with the incidents. Between my job and running into dishonest people, I began to wonder if I was cursed.

I have never truly loved a man. I have cared for men such as Eldrin, Andrew and Steffen. But did I love them? The answer to the question is an emphatic NO! However, I admit that I am a paradox wrapped in an enigma with a question mark as the crowning bow.

"Woo, did I ever tell you about the time I went to jail?"

"Nawh. Your little ass was in jail? I know you were scared."

"You ought to know the feeling," I said while laughing.

"OOOOOO, Father! I went one time and that was for a DUI. What your ass went for?"

"I'm getting ready to tell you 'bout it."

I was the only child out of the nine in my family who ever went to jail. I went to jail fucking with a tenant who told a lie on me. She claimed that I had a knife. I did not. She lied. She and her sister were getting ready to whip my ass. So, I picked up a big stick to defend myself. I told them to get back. I waved the stick as I walked to my car. As soon as I got in my car, police came from everywhere and nowhere at the same time. There were at least four or five police cars. Don't let me leave out that her sister was the mayor of this little town. So, I really didn't have a chance. The charge was assault with a deadly weapon. There was no "deadly weapon" anywhere to be found. Was I wrong to try to protect myself from an ass-whipping? I say no, but the fact remained that I ended up in jail. That bitch conveniently forgot to mention that she and her sister were getting ready to whip my ass. I remained in a holding cell for twenty four hours. It was indeed a nightmare from Hell.

I was so depressed and scared that I was gonna lose my job because I was charged with a felony. I attempted suicide for the second time in my life. The only difference was that I used sleeping pills. The last thing I remembered was calling my sister. I told her that I didn't want to live anymore. There were some things that happened to me in jail that I care to never talk about. When I woke up, I was in the hospital. My stomach had been pumped. I was cuffed to the bed. My sister Rebeca's face was the first thing I saw when I opened my eyes. If it wasn't for my psychologist, who came to the hospital at an ungodly hour to sign my release form, I would have been hauled off to a mental institution. Thank God she was on call that night.

"I'm so glad God kept you here. Molly, PLEASE don't ever do that again," Woo said in a sad tone.

"I'm not, Woo."

"Promise me now," Woo insisted.

"Woo…I promise you."

My mother's health deteriorated rapidly between 1994 and 2003. She had a stroke in 1994 that left her paralyzed on her right side and her speech impaired. As a testament to her strength and character, my mother fought back from the awful effects of the stroke and lived almost ten more wonderful years.

A couple of days before my mother passed away, I had to come home to Valletta to get some papers. Then, I got right back on the road to Alabama. As soon as I got upstairs, I smelled shit. It was painted all over my door, as though someone had used a paintbrush. I called the police. They came out and investigated. The police found the culprit. It was my psychotic neighbor. The neighbor confessed to the police that he had shit-painted my doorway because my dog had shitted in his yard. This was not true because I never took my dog anywhere near his crazy-ass door. We lived in condominiums. Nobody personally owned a yard. He forgot to mention that his flamingly gay neighbor had a dog. In addition, we lived in two buildings separated by a partition.

The police officers came to me and said, "Ms., he admitted to doing it and is willing to clean your door or buy you a new one." I told both of the officers, "Hell, naw! My mother is in Alabama on the verge of passing away, and I had to come home to find SHIT on my door? I don't think so. His monkey ass is going to jail tonight!" They didn't want to do the report, so I asked to speak with their superior officer. This request made them write the report. They handcuffed this psychopath and took him in. I had to go to the police department to file charges. This took at least four hours. This was four hours that I could have been with mother, instead of dealing with this bullshit. He was later found guilty and was sentenced to clean both the Humane Society and the public transit vehicles.

"Dude was crazy as hell," Woo said.

"Hell, yeah! He was crazy and stupid for even admitting to doing something that psychotic."

I drove back to Alabama that morning at five o'clock with no sleep to speak of. It was the month of August, so it was extremely hot outside. The fog was so thick that I could hardly see the lines on the road. Finally, I made it home. I rushed to my mama's bedside.

"Mama." I found strength enough to say.

"It's me, Molly. I'm here." Her eyes opened. She seemed to have been waiting on me.

"Don't die. Mama, Please don't die," I pleaded.

I sat at mama's bedside. I told her about what had just happened. I would always let her know about what was going on with me. She barely had her eyes open. She couldn't talk. I knew what she was thinking. Baby, what have you gotten into, now? I promised her that morning, that no matter what, I was gonna try my best to stay out of trouble.

I said, "Mama, you know it's always been something with me. I don't always bring things on myself. Problems just follow me. Why? I don't know. I promise you, mama, that I'm gonna try to avoid any type of confusion. I promise you," I said crying. "Mama, you don't have to worry about me. I'll be alright. I know you've been worrying 'bout me all your life. Mama, I'm a big girl, now. I can take care of myself. So, don't worry about me."

Tears were flowing down my face. Deep down I knew that I wasn't a big girl at all. I was still somewhat immature. I was still that same adolescent who did things before thinking. What was I gonna do without mama? My baby sister Allison put her arm on my shoulder. I lowered my head to catch a breath. My chest was so damn tight. I was grasping for air. The tears that streaked down my face felt like drops of hot water. I watched my mother take her last breath. JESUS, JESUS, JESUS, help me! is all I could say.

My baby sister said, "Molly, she's still with us. She always will be. Please don't cry. Whenever you need to see mama, just look in the mirror."

While my mother was lying in the funeral home, I heard that bitch, Jene, and my daddy's new ho, Velma, who was yet another member of the Stanfordson family, had gone by to view her body. I was so mad. I told Deputy McDaniel that if they showed up at the funeral, it was gonna be a fight right there in the church. I meant each and every word.

"I can't believe they had the nerve," Woo stated.

"Please believe it. Woo, it would have been hell to pay 'cause I was gonna show out and kick their ass."

My daddy cried the day of the funeral. Given the way that he treated my mother, I never imagined he would have reacted that way. All I could think of was just standing up and popping him in the back of his fucking head because of how he had cheated on my mother. I was suffering and angry at the same time. None of my so-called friends, not even Paula herself, showed up to support me. Because of the grief and lack of emotional support, I eventually had to receive professional help from a psychiatrist. If it wasn't for this help, my faith in God, and my dog Minnie Bell, I don't know what I would have done.

Even to this day, there are times when her absence hits me and I shed tears. Those tears most often come at night as I try to sleep. My pillow is my silent confidante as it receives all of my tears. Some mornings, I feel like it was just a bad dream and that mama is still at home. I attempt to dial her number, but reality sets in. I wish my mother was still here. I miss her more than words or emotions can describe. I love her so much. I sometimes ask, "Why, mama? Why did God have to take you? Why?"

I find myself remembering the times I combed her long pretty hair. I recall the sound of her laughter, the way she held me and told me I was beautiful and special. These were comforting memories.

"Your mama was so sweet. I'm glad that I got a chance to meet her. I'm so sorry, Molly," Woo said while sniffling.

I'm so glad I listened to God and my inner spirit back in 2001 and named my dog Minnie Bell. This was the name on the social security card that mama received in the mail back in 1984. It said Minnie Bell, instead of her given name. From then on, I called her Minnie Bell. She started to answer to it. Eventually, everybody else in the family started calling her Minnie Bell.

I remember back in 2001, I called mama and said, "Mama, guess what? I got a puppy and I named her Minnie Bell." She laughed and laughed. Everybody fell in love with my little doggie. Now, it seems like Minnie Bell is always getting into something, like I did as a child. Cute and full of herself, she is the canine version of her owner. Minnie Bell is a comfort for me. She helps ease the pain.

After I finally recovered from my relationship with Paula, I met my so-called next real girlfriend Heidi, whose nickname was Summer. I met her at a nightclub. We had been dating at least a year prior to my mom's passing. I could tell from the moment we met that she was a stripper. Summer had 38 DD breasts that complemented an already gorgeous body overall and a beautiful face. Everywhere she went, there would be heads turning as one would expect. Because of this, she never took any other vocation seriously. She only stripped one week out of a month. She made enough in seven days to cover a month's worth of expenses.

During this time, I was dealing with my mother's death. Summer didn't make the situation easier. She wanted to come to Alabama to my mom's funeral, but I insisted that she not. I needed to be alone with my family. All she wanted to do was argue. All the fighting negated the fact that we had a good sex life. That fact neutralized the times when I tried to break up with Summer, as she would call to apologize, and then we ended up having sex. The cycle repeated itself several times over our tumultuous three year relationship. I couldn't say the same for Summer. I had a confrontation with her the week after my mother's funeral because I was tired of the stripping. I just got tired of her sorry ass, in general.

"What happened?" Woo asked.

We were watching television; she decided that she wanted to order Chinese food.

I asked, "Are you paying for it?"

She said, "Baby, you know I don't have a job."

This shit snapped a nerve in me.

"Why don't you go out and get a real job?" I asked in a tone which did not lend itself to civil conversation.

"What I need a real job for?"

"Ain't you tired of being a ho?" I asked angrily.

"Your mama was a ho!"

Before I realized what I was doing, I grabbed my gun from inside of my entertainment unit and withdrew it from its holster. We struggled. I dropped the gun to prevent it from going off. With that, I also dropped my defenses. We ended up making fiery love. What a ludicrous outcome to such a heated confrontation. That was just the nature of our relationship. I got tired of the drama and broke up with her.

"So, you stayed with her for TWO MORE YEARS, after she called your mother a whore and you had to draw your pistol on her?" Woo asked incredulously.

"What can I say? The reason that I stayed with her was because the sex was good, I guess. I'm just being honest with you," I said.

All we did was fuck and eat and argue and fuck. We fucked everywhere. In the movie theater, the back seat, front seat, restaurants, and in public restrooms. One time, we fucked on her roommate's dinner table. She was the "turkey". That's just the truth. I'm telling you things 'bout me that you never knew.

I gained twenty pounds within two months after Summer and I broke up.

"Right now, you know more 'bout me than anyone here on earth," I said.

"It's true. Sex does keep the weight down," Woo giggled.

{ CHAPTER 7 }

Blood Money

Around the end of 2002, this black hen at the post office caused me a lot of problems. She harassed the hell out of me. She harassed everyone that she didn't like. My supervisor had by far the most Equal Employment Opportunity Commission (EEOC) complaints filed against her, more than any other supervisor in the region. No one in upper management wanted to help me. I mentioned to my co-worker Maggie that I needed an attorney, but it was hard to find one with balls enough to go up against the Federal Government.

Maggie said, "One of my friends used to work for the EEOC within the postal service. He has knowledge of the EEOC process."

"Is he a lawyer?"

"No, but he is very familiar with the EEOC process."

I asked Maggie for this person's phone number.

She said, "First, I have to check with him. Then, I'll get back with you."

I got her friend's number a few days later and called him.

"Molly, why is it that you seem to have so much trouble with your managers, especially the females? That's all I ever hear you talk about when you speak 'bout your job. It's always negative stuff," Woo said with disgust.

"For one thing, the postal service has their in-house EEOC branch. This is separate from the other national organization. They have almost everything in-house. This is why it's so hard to fight them. They have judges downtown who generally rule in their favor in grievances. Well, this one particular female supervisor where I work cares more about harassing the workers than getting the public's mail out on time," I said.

"Don't you have a damn union?" Woo asked.

"Yup, but most of the local union stewards are weak-ass fuckers. The weak outnumber the strong. Maybe, one day, we'll get a strong leader," I replied.

"What about the Postmaster General? Doesn't he care about managers focusing on bullshit games rather than doing their job?" Woo asked.

I steered her away from this line of questioning.

"Let's get back to Maggie. We've gotten off the subject," I said.

The man's name was Thomas Walters. What a pleasant voice on the other end of the phone, I thought. I heard such a caring tone in his conversation. I explained to him in detail about how my supervisor was harassing me. He mentioned to me that his wife also had a complaint with the EEOC. He claimed her supervisor had assaulted her and that she required medical attention afterwards. I spoke with his wife, Phyllis, over the phone briefly. I only asked her a couple of questions. At the time, she was a union representative in the district where she worked. I can still hear her voice crystal clear in my head, from the cadence of her words right down to the tone and nuances of her gravelly voice.

Thomas met with me at my home to discuss my case further. He was as impressed with my home as I was depressed about my situation. Thomas talked about my home as if he had never seen anything in his life that was nice. I really didn't care about his compliments because they were irrelevant to my situation.

I'm hurting man; so, shut the fuck up. I wanted to say that so badly. Can't your fat ass see the frustration on my face? Let's get on with the EEOC conversation. I know you heard it over the phone. That's why you are here now. Shut the fuck up p-l-e-a-s-e!

Finally, the telepathic message that I sent him must have worked because he shut up. We began to talk about the government. I mentioned my prior EEOC complaints and went into detail about them. He wrote on a notepad as I spoke. I became more and more impressed as we conversed. He asked all of the right questions. I never had to repeat myself. It seemed as though he understood the situation as I went along. The last thing I needed was to be aggravated by some person who didn't really know the EEOC process or who wanted to use me to gain their experience.

Thomas listened to me when I told him that I was so sick and depressed over the harassment. I spoke of having no peace of mind for days and no sleep. I intimated that the situation was so taxing that I threw up constantly. I couldn't eat. I cried all the time. Thomas made me feel as though he was the only person in the world who understood my pain. He kept reminding me that Phyllis was going through some of what I was going through. He said that she threw up frequently also. She was sick and depressed all of the time. The next day, Thomas called my managers. He also called the lead manager. He called everybody. Thomas really cares about me, I thought.

The calls to upper management didn't do any damn good. Thomas told me that he was gonna write the EEOC for the first process and that he wanted to meet with me to sign the complaint. First, he wanted me to proofread it. I met him a couple days later at the Quick Trip convenience store around the corner from the building where I worked to proofread the document. Thomas got into my car. The first thing he started to talk about was my Lexus. Oh shit! How long is this gonna go on?

"Well, how does a person work for the government, drive a Lexus, and live in a penthouse on Devonshire Drive?" Thomas asked.

Devonshire was a prominent area in South Georgia. I took a deep breath and thought. Damn, that's a good question. In the back of my mind, I knew how individuals thought. They thought black prosperity usually equaled some kind of illicit activity. I revealed my secret weapon to him so that he would give me the fucking papers to sign. The secret was the dot-com days. I needed to speed things along since I was almost running late for work. He already knew more than enough about me for only having known me for a few days.

Finally, I got to read the complaint. I was so amazed by his writing skills that I became very optimistic. In the back of my mind, I was saying to myself, Wow, this is brilliant! Thomas took down every word that I said that first day. He even added to my words, thereby, creating the best EEOC complaint I had ever seen written.

Dot Belgrave could not have written a better complaint. Dot was an attorney out of Philadelphia, Pennsylvania. She had won many EEOC cases against the government. She was one of the best attorneys who handled EEOC cases against the federal government. She worked on a case for me back in 1996 against the government. We were so sure that the case was a winner. She didn't even charge any upfront fees, not even when she flew to Georgia or when the case was delayed. There were two delays during the case. She did not charge either time. This was how sure she was of the outcome in our favor. Even though we didn't win, Dot's professionalism left an indelible impression on me.

In light of the similarly stellar impression that Thomas had made on me with his literary skill, I signed the complaint. He said that he would send it certified mail the next day. I gave him the money to mail the document. He never really mentioned any other money. He did say that I would probably win my retaliation complaint and receive monetary damages. In subsequent conversations, Thomas began to tell me about the attorney that Phyllis had named Billy. He said that Billy would take cases on a contingency basis.

I asked, "What would happen if he doesn't take the case?"

He said, "He has Phyllis's case and I can talk him into taking yours."

As long as I win my case, it didn't matter who defended me. However, I was under the impression that Thomas was gonna take my EEOC complaint from beginning to end based upon our conversations. I should have known better. Well, at least,

I was satisfied with the beginning of my dealings with him. I felt relatively comfortable around Thomas, but I always tried to keep the conversation geared toward what we were meeting for. He tried to talk about other things like my dog or my condo or my car. I stayed focused on the job, which was the complaint that I were filing. Eventually all mentioning of the ballyhooed "Billy" ceased completely.

The truth of the situation was I had absorbed my supervisor into my skin, literally. That whore was always on my mind! My supervisor was in my dreams. Actually, they were nightmares. There was some real shit going on! I really didn't want to talk about anything else other than my job and how my supervisor kept fucking with me everyday. I must have had a big sign on my head that read 'Please fuck with me.' We didn't go to mediation in my case. Thomas actually seemed paranoid over going to mediation with me.

He said, "It might mess up Phyllis's case."

I asked, "How could it mess up her case? We're two totally separate circumstances."

Thomas said, "The government inspectors will come and harass me at my house. They will try to make me stop representing you."

That whole theory was out in space, but he was convinced of that so-called truth.

"You should have known right then that he was crazy. He sounds likes Mr. Brooks," Woo stated.

"You're right. I should have suspected something. Who the hell is Mr. Brooks? Is that Hawk's last name? You know the dude that whips your ass all the time," I sniggled.

"Never mind, we ain't fixing to go there! He's just somebody crazy. You can go on with the story," Woo said.

Thomas began to tell me about the cases he read while he

worked at EEOC. This is the same branch of the federal government that he now fought. He told me about one case where a manager actually raped several women. He called certain females into his office and forced them to perform oral sex on him. Many of those women suffered nervous breakdowns because of the horrible things that were done to them. During the investigations, Thomas alleged that the same manager was simply transferred to another location. This slime ball of a supervisor supposedly did the same thing to several different females over a period of years.

Thomas said, "None of those females knew of each other because the government would settle the cases in secret. The manager was moved and no one knew the real reason. The manager kept doing the same thing over and over and the government just kept moving him. The government inspectors would just break into people homes for no just cause. One morning, Phyllis and I woke up to find all four tires on both cars flattened. We knew the postal inspectors did it."

"Did you call the police?"

He responded, "No, we just got new tires."

I said emphatically, "You should have called and made a complaint. Not calling the police over that kind of vandalism doesn't make sense!"

Thomas didn't say anything to that statement. I felt so sorry for him and Phyllis at that point. It was on my mind the rest of the night! The postal service should not do that to that poor man and his family. My heart wept for him and Phyllis. At the time, there was no way on Earth for me to know that Thomas was a liar.

"You must have had a pretty good record to get a transfer from West Palm to Valletta, right?" Woo asked.

"Hell, naw! The problem with Postal Service transfers was that generally they don't grant them unless you have a damn good record," I stated, "I had to get closer to my mother 'cause it was too taxing for me to drive from Florida to Alabama. I had to find a way and I did. I used the best means that I had at my disposal," I said.

"Let me guess. Your solution probably involved using sex in some form," Woo joked.

"Of course, it did."

"Was it a man or a woman that you pussy whipped?" Woo asked.

"Okay, first of all, don't judge me 'cause I did what I had to do. Woo, sometimes you do bad things for good reasons. This time I did a questionable thing for the best reason in the world. I lucked up and got an interview with a white manager who loved black women."

"He loved black women, meaning?" Woo asked with a leading tone.

"Meaning, he wanted some of this pussy. So, I gave him some to get what I needed," I said. "What's wrong with that?" I asked. "We, women have been using pussy for years to get what we need and men keep paying the price, right?" I laughed.

"So, you fucked a white man to get the transfer," she stated. "Did he break the stereotype, too?"

"Hell, yeah, he did! That white man-little dick, black man-big dick myth is bullshit!" I cracked.

"Girl, you love wiggers, don't you?"

"What's that?" I asked.

"A 'wigger' is a white nigger. He has to have a black man's swagger to be called that. He was probably just a white man with a big dick. Was it worth it?"

"I didn't give a damn 'bout how good or bad it was, Woo! Hell, I needed to be closer to my mama. Sex was taking so long with ol' dude that I had to fake an orgasm."

"I heard that," Woo said defiantly.

"Okay, can we get back on track, now? We're getting closer to what this crazy ass bastard did to his wife," I stated. "First, I need to tell you a little more 'bout the EEOC case so that you fully understand the entire picture.. We have been talking all night and you still ain't heard the real shit."

"This must be some tripping shit!" Woo said.

"I'll let you be the judge of that," I replied.

****

I had my EEOC complaint in process at the same time my mother's health was failing. I requested a revised work schedule. I wanted to work and help my sister take care of my mother, but it was denied. I decided the hell with them. I took off for the rest of the time that I needed. It didn't matter how long of a leave it was gonna be because nothing was going to keep me from being with her. The federal government kept me from going to my Granddaddy Jake's funeral back in 1988. At that time, I didn't know any better. I had gotten an official discussion on my attendance and the next step was a letter or reprimand. I was too scared to take off from work and go to my own granddaddy's funeral.

"I can't believe they wouldn't let you off knowing your mama was really sick," Woo said slowly.

"That's what I've been telling you. They do shit to employees just to make them miserable!" I screamed. "Hell, I wasn't lying to you earlier nor was I bullshitting you."

"Damn, that's really hard to believe," Woo said.

"Well, you best believe it 'cause it's the damn truth!"

"I've lived with that decision every day because I loved my grandfather. I should have just taken off regardless of the consequences," I said.

"That's just pure evil," Woo said in a low tone.

During the time my mama was on her death bed, I made a couple of promises to her. One was concerning the job. I knew how my mother felt about me filing complaints on the job. For that reason, I promised that I would drop the EEOC complaint and any other grievances. I kept my promise to my mother for nearly three years. I worked very hard at trying to get along with my supervisor. Let the truth be told. I had no energy to fight.

Thomas and I didn't talk for years after that initial encounter. Nevertheless, I kept his telephone number, just in case I needed him in the future. If I could have foreseen that future, I would have flushed his number down the toilet.

"Yeah, girl. You should have burned it using 93% octane!" Woo said.

I returned to work after being out on leave because I was assaulted. Two females had beaten me severely in the hallway of my building. The principal assailant was arrested and charged; yet, the damage had already taken its toll on me. I was on a shift known as tour one. I came in at 11:00 PM and got off at 7:30 AM. This shift wasn't working for me, so I put in a revised schedule. The traffic was heavy traveling to downtown Valletta. My new hours were 12:00 AM to 8:30 AM. Now, this schedule was much better for me. I came to work every night on time for at least two weeks. Then, the same supervisor started to fuck with me. She was the day shift supervisor and her reporting time was 7:00 AM. She really should not have had any contact with me, but she made it her business to find me every morning and page me throughout the building.

"Was it the black hen?" Woo asked.

"Yup, girl you crazy!" I started laughing. "Seventy percent of the supervisors are black hens where I work."

"What happened to the white manager that gave you the transfer?" Woo asked.

"They sent his ass somewhere, who knows?"

"No wonder the shit is fucked up there!" Woo chuckled.

"Woo, you're probably right!"

This particular HEN started to turn the other managers against me. They were weak-minded individuals. They all gradually changed their ways toward me. I felt like a leper.

One morning around seven o'clock, I re-injured my back while lifting heavy trays of mail. I sat at a table and tried to get myself together. I cried a flood of tears because of the pain. The HEN approached me requesting that I report to an area which was against my restrictions. I was crying so damn hard. I was in pain from hell, but that didn't deter her.

She said, "Report to the area!"

"I'm really in a lot of pain," I said, while sniffling through my tears. "Can I just sit here at the table?"

She said, "I'm instructing you to report to the area!"

"I need to go to the hospital."

"Go to the manager's office," she said.

"Molly, sounds like she wanted you to eat her pussy," Woo laughed out loud.

"She wasn't my type, my dear," I said flatly.

"Yeah, I know your type. Light- skinned with long hair,"

Woo said.

"That's not necessarily true. Paula wasn't light-skinned nor did she have long hair. So, kiss my ass, bitch!" I laughed. "Stop interrupting me. You're making me laugh too much. This shit is serious!"

"Okay, I can't make any promises. Will you please get to the murder part?" Woo asked.

I went to the office and waited for a supervisor to take me to the hospital. They finally found someone to do the paperwork, so I could be treated for my injuries. The supervisor was very hostile to me in front of everybody while all of this was transpiring. I was in too much pain to respond to her ignorance. They waited until ten in the morning, before deciding to take me to the hospital. I was dropped off.

"They waited that long to take you to the hospital, Why?" Woo asked.

"It's just another form of harassment," I responded.

While at home, I thought about the entire ordeal and decided that I was treated wrongfully. I wasn't going back to work under that monster. It was too stressful. I also thought about the promises to my mother. I got on my knees and asked her to forgive me. I couldn't let them get away with this!

I called Thomas after not having spoken with him in nearly three years. I discussed the situation thoroughly with him. He said that he would come over to my house and go over the EEOC claim with me. During the conversation, Thomas casually mentioned that Phyllis had passed away earlier in the year. I felt a sense of grief for him. We then set up a date to meet once more. He came by and took very detailed notes just like before.

When he got ready to leave, he said, "I'll call you once I've completed the papers. I'm only charging you four hundred dollars to process the paperwork and go to mediation." It all seemed fair, so I wrote him a check. Thomas called a few days later and gave me directions to his office. I went there to expedite matters.

Once I arrived at his shop, I was quite impressed with the decorations and the general set-up. It looked as if Thomas had achieved a level of success based on his surroundings. His affiliation with Georgia Upholstery contributed to the ambience. Thomas was one of the principal owners of Georgia Upholstery, which carried a variety of furniture for the home and office. He had two part-time workers, Britney and Tracey. Britney was at the shop on the day I stopped by. I signed the EEOC papers.

"So, Thomas went from working temporary at the postal service to fixing furniture? Oh, my! What a dream!" Woo said.

"It was a 'how can I sit on my fat ass' dream," I quipped.

My co-worker, Celestine Martin, was familiar with the EEOC process within the postal service. So, I put Thomas in contact with her via my cell phone. In my mind, I wanted to create a 'dream team.' Thomas and Celestine were the perfect match. Thomas finished up the call with Celestine. Ten minutes later, he said, "Celestine is not a paralegal. She's a postal inspector."

"Thomas just wanted all of the money for himself. He knew Celestine wasn't no damn postal inspector. That was just plain ol' bullshit!" Woo said in a loud tone.

All night I pondered the possibility that I was misinformed. Celestine couldn't be a postal inspector! I took it all for what it was worth. I forgot about the dream team and just resigned myself to Thomas handling the case on his own. I was 100% convinced that Celestine was not a government inspector.

Thomas is just having a hard time dealing with Phyllis' death, I said to myself. I remembered him saying something about the inspectors flattening his tires. I believed it was just paranoia on his part.

Before I left the shop, we decided to get something to eat. We ate at a place he was familiar with called Polazzo's. It was authentic Italian cuisine. For this meal, I pick up the tab, which was relatively costly. The second time, he paid for some cheap meal at a local deli. I keep referring to it as a cheap meal because the meal I provided for him was around forty dollars, while the second meal couldn't have been more than ten dollars total. During the second meal, I mentioned my idea for a modeling agency. At first, I was a little reluctant, but Thomas kept asking me about my idea. Finally, I relented. I went over the idea detail by detail. I wanted a modeling agency devoted to undiscovered beauties in the South Georgia area. I knew the concept would sell if it got enough exposure. I needed grants for small businesses. I also needed someone to write the grant proposals. At first, he didn't seem overly interested in the modeling concept at all. However, the next day, I got a call from Thomas. He said, "I thought about your idea and I think it's great. Can you come by the office?"

"How could he know about a modeling agency? He runs an upholstery shop." Woo said with disgust.

"Remember I told you how good his writing skills were? Well, I needed a writer to put together grant proposals."

"Ummm. I would have gotten someone that worked in that area of expertise. Not someone who fixed furniture," Woo replied with a forceful tone.

This is when I met Tracey for the first time. We were all sitting around the table. Thomas's main concern was a name for the modeling agency. He wanted it to be 'The Modeling Shop'.

Now, I should have known that something wasn't right with that picture, but I ignored the signs. I had already told him that I wanted it to be called 'Ten Cents Modeling Agency.' I told him that I chose this name because of Chyna, my friend who was killed. I wanted to keep her dream alive.

I'll never forget the day I received the news of her death. I had gone out of town for the weekend. When I got back to work on that Monday, a co-worker ran up to me. She asked if I had heard about Chyna. I was thinking she done made it big all of a sudden. My co-worker informed me that she had been killed in a car accident over the weekend. Hell, I nearly fainted. I cried for months. Thomas asked Britney and Tracey what they thought about various names.

"Wait a minute! Wait a minute! Why would he ask two young girls, that don't know shit about modeling, their opinion?!" Woo screamed.

"That's what I was thinking, too."

I sat and listened for two damn hours. It was getting dark. I knew I wasn't gonna make it home by dark. That was a problem. I told Thomas about my religious beliefs. After I declared my religion, Thomas declared he was Jewish. The only black Jew I've ever heard of was Sammy Davis Jr., but I gave Thomas the benefit of the doubt. Finally fed up with the useless brainstorming, I declared to them all that the modeling agency would be called 'Ten Cents' and nothing else. I didn't see why we were even having the conversation. It was my idea and it had absolutely nothing to do with my EEOC case. It was taking up valuable time. I was agitated. Possibly to reinforce his claim, he demonstrated how he could write my name in Hebrew. He wrote something on a piece of paper in a script I'd never seen before. To this day, I don't know whether or not it was a real or made up lie. My bets are on the lie. Who gives a shit about all of this, I thought.

"Wait a minute. He said that he was a Jew? Girl, you know damn well that bastard was lying!" Woo laughed.

"Yeah, he was lying through his ugly ass mug. I try to give everyone a chance, though."

"I'm sorry to interrupt you, but that was a clear lie," Woo said.

"Hey, my guardian angels were giving me signs, but I ignored them," I sighed.

"He's probably an Atheist!" Woo chuckled.

"I try not to question any man's religion. I'll leave that alone."

All the signs were there. Little angels were on my shoulders, whispering into my ear and telling me to be careful. I wasn't paying attention.

After we finished discussing possible names for the modeling agency, Britney and Tracey left the office. This is when Thomas asked me to tell him about Chyna.

"I wouldn't have told him SHIT!" Woo said in a forceful tone.

I told him the full story about how I had met Chyna and eventually asked her to move in with me. She was going to accept, but she met her untimely death. I told Thomas all of this. I allowed him a level of intimacy that he was not worthy of. However, he began to tell me some personal things about himself. Most interesting of what he revealed was that he was thinking about marrying an African woman he had met on the internet.

I asked, "Have you guys met in person?"

I wondered if she had seen his big, ugly ass. If so, why would she still want to marry him? She had to be ugly herself or looking for a green card.

He said, "We hadn't met. She lost her husband to cancer. So, we have a lot in common."

"Thomas, I'm sure you're not finished grieving over Phyllis, yet. Chyna died back in March and I still think about her," I said.

"Well, wherever she is right now, I know that Phyllis would be happy for me to move on," he said, appearing to stifle back tears.

"What about your social security payments? Are they enough to supplement your income?" I asked.

"I only get fourteen hundred dollars a month," he said while staring at the wall.

"You do know that your benefits will stop if you marry again, right?"

"I guess it depends on whether or not she's worth it," Thomas said in a rather businesslike tone.

The signs were there and they started to mount up. It seemed as if there was an angel and a devil on my shoulder. One told me to turn tail and run. The other said to stay and listen.

"Thomas, what about the kids. How do they feel? Have you mentioned it to your kids?"

"I really hadn't talked with them in depth about it," he said.

"Do you get any help from the mother of your oldest kid?"

"No, I don't receive any support for him. His mother is dead too," he responded, with a sad and despondent tone.

I was too sorry to hear about the tragedies in his life. So, I left the subject alone. Damn, those bitches at the post office killed Phyllis! That was all I could think about while he lamented. I also mentioned my lawsuit against the condominium complex where I lived. I told him the full story about how the gateman let two young women in without my permission. They waited for me in my hallway. They ambushed and beat the hell out of me. There was so much going on at that time in my life.

"Why are two women always attacking you? It was two in school, the two who were your tenants, and, now, them two HOES!" Woo chuckled.

I told Thomas the story about the particular female who assaulted me. I told him about how I had mentioned to her that I wasn't looking for a relationship when I first met her. I was still grieving over Chyna. I told him about the crazy signs I started to recognized. She lied about her age. At first, she told me she was twenty-one. She had an ID picture with her that told the same. I later saw a basket in her apartment filled with nothing but fake ID's. The reality was that she was nineteen. As I was telling Thomas the story, I began to feel a little skeptical about whether or not he was even listening. It seemed like his mind was on another subject.

"What were the crazy signs you saw?" Woo asked.

"One Thursday afternoon, the girl called me to ask if she could go to Bible study with me. I didn't mind, so I picked her up from the train station. Once we got to the church, I happened to look down at her black bag and notice it was moving. I asked her why her bag was moving. She responded, 'Oh, that's just my dog.' I hurried up and took her ass home."

"You are lying for real!" Woo started laughing.

"I'm for real. No lie."

We both laughed.

"Molly, I know you too well. Now, why didn't you like this girl? Tell the truth," Woo demanded.

"We were simply a bad match. She was fake from head to toe with fake breasts and a fake ass. Apparently, she had a back alley bootleg plastic surgeon," I said. "No real professional would have done such shabby work."

"I knew it had to be another reason. Girl, I know you!" Woo giggled.

"I guess you THINK you know me, huh?" We both laughed.

Thomas's fat ass then went on to talk about how, when he was in college, he had a friend who experienced being with another male. I didn't say shit while he went into this diatribe. As it became monotonous and invasive, I cut all answers short. With all of the questions he asked, I can honestly say that this was the first time I felt so uncomfortable over the subject of my sexuality. For the most part, I simply let him do most of the talking. I tried steering the conversation toward another subject, but he would bring everything back to the subject of my sexuality. He even said that his mother was open-minded to different things. I cut the conversation short again! It seemed like this bastard was trying to come on to me. I don't have anything against fat men as a rule since I've had my share of big men and big women. The difference was the women were sexy and big, as well as with pretty faces.

"So, you're talking 'bout big and shapely like Monique?" Woo laughed.

"Yeah, I like Monique. Hell, she's big and sexy with it!" I responded.

This is why I felt so damn uncomfortable. Every time I took a look at him, he looked more and more like Caesar from the movie "The Planet of the Apes". To me, Thomas's face looked like a gorilla's face and that was an accurate assessment. One thing I didn't want to do was make him feel upset. I knew I needed him to answer my questions involving EEOC.

Thomas phoned me the next day to converse with me about

the modeling agency. He was hyping it up to be something potentially great. This kind of pep talk was just what I wanted to hear at that time. He wanted to take the lead. He proposed that he become the assistant manager.

He said, "I'll be responsible for keeping the records and getting investors. I'll write all the grant proposals."

I wanted to hear positive feedback from my potential grant writer. He would be the one writing the majority of the proposals. I needed him to make this dream of mine, as well as Chyna's, come true.

"You should have left that fat bull fixing furniture!" Woo said. "How can he magically transform from repairing furniture to being a manager for your agency?!" Woo hollered.

"Woo, just shut up!" I said.

I was fighting depression like I was in a war!

At the end of a very lengthy conversation, Thomas asked, "Would you like to spend New Year's Eve over at my mother's house? I'm making gumbo for all of us," he said.

Thomas knew through our conversations that gumbo was my favorite dish. I was excited because I had no plans for the holidays, but I would only attend with one condition — that I bring my dog.

Thomas said, "Oh, I love Minnie Bell. She's my favorite dog."

I could not see it clearly at the time, but Thomas seemed to be calculatingly saying and doing all of the right things.

He said, "I need to OK it with my mother first."

I replied, "If your mother doesn't like dogs, I completely understand."

He responded, "Let me call you back in a couple of minutes."

He called back and said it wasn't a problem. This was yet

another sign that I was given, which I ignored. If his mother cared for dogs as Thomas had claimed, he wouldn't have had to get her to OK anything. The truth of the matter was his mother probably didn't like dogs. He probably told her that he had a plan for me and that it required her cooperation. Part of the scheme was for him to make me feel as comfortable as possible. His mother, of course, went along with him and so did his oldest son. I didn't realize it at the time, but again my guardian angels were giving me signs through my skepticism that I continually ignored.

"Neither one of those boys have a mama? Damn!" Woo screamed.

Previously, I told Thomas that I didn't eat pork. So, he made sure to buy turkey sausage. Whatever I wanted in the gumbo was what he put in it. New Year's Eve finally came. Minnie Bell and I met Thomas in front of his mother's house. He invited me in and I met the oldest son, Barry. He was a light-skinned boy. He was around thirteen with gray eyes. Thomas spoke glowingly of that child as though he was his prized possession. Thomas gushed over Barry. It seemed as though he was most proud of the way Barry looked and ashamed of the younger son, Little T. I asked him earlier that week which side of the family Barry got the gray eyes from.

He said, "He got them from my mother's side of the family."

He explained that his grandmother or one of her ancestors had gray eyes. He told me that his grandmother was raped by her own brother and went on to say that his mother was raped and impregnated in college by a white professor. This man would have been Thomas's father. Thomas didn't, however, look like he was bi-racial at all. He spilled his family secrets. Then, all of a sudden, he stopped talking. He started crying. I believed everything he told me.

"Do you think that his mom was raped?" Woo asked softly.

"You know, I just don't know," I answered obligingly.

Then, I met little T. He was a brown-skinned little boy. I sensed that he had a lot of anger simmering on a low boil within him. He constantly whined throughout the day. He was rude. It's not normal for a child around his age to be mean and indifferent to a little dog, but he shunned Minnie Bell every time she attempted to play with him. Then, I met Thomas's mother. She was nothing like Thomas described. She was not unpleasant, but I could sense a little deception going on in her speech and in her mannerisms. His mother tried to appear cordial, yet it was strained. It was as though she was forced into acting nice. Once again, I continued to ignore the signs. Next, a short man came downstairs. Thomas introduced him as his mother's fiancé. Later, another man came downstairs. Thomas introduced him as his uncle. Earlier that week, Thomas mentioned that his uncle lived with him.

He said, "He gets on my nerves because he won't wash his hands after he goes to the bathroom."

I asked, "How do you know whether or not he washes his hands?"

He answered, "I listen for running water."

"Well, I'll be a monkey's uncle! Should NA bitch been sleep?" Woo hissed.

This was yet another sign I ignored. He was unusually deceptive and invasive of people's privacy to a degree that went past normal. I couldn't see this at the time. In retrospect, it was all too clear. The last time Thomas came by my house, he was impressed with my library. One of the books he was especially impressed with was titled "The Prince" by Niccolo

Machiavelli. We were sitting in his mother's living room watching television when Barry started talking about that particular book. Thomas obviously coached him prior to my arrival, telling him to mention the book and act as though he had read it. Thomas hoped that Barry's diverse literary catalog of reading would impress me. From a rear-view mirror's view, everything was clearly set up. I had no clue.

"I feel sorry for the woman that marries his oldest son. He's gonna be a lot like his father, huh?" Woo asked with concern.

"Yup," I responded.

There I was in the presence of what seemed to be one big, jovial, and close-knit family. They were very well-spoken individuals. They were probably all coached. Their verbs all fell neatly into place. To the casual observer, it seemed that they all got along so well. Whenever I was in the presence of my family members, they always seemed to be screaming and yelling. They were such a perfect family that they reminded me of a television sitcom. It was only a minute later that I heard an argument break out in the kitchen. It was Thomas and his mother. I sat and thought, Wow, I can't believe he's arguing with his mother. They were talking to each other as if they wanted to fight. The oldest son spoke out and reminded them that they had company. The argument subsided after Gray Eyes spoke up. This was yet another harbinger of what was to come. Thomas invited me to come to the table and take a seat. We began to eat dinner. I said my grace before beginning to eat as I always did. I didn't see any of them doing the same. Not necessarily a sign but food for thought, pardon the pun. If you wanna know the truth, the so-called gumbo wasn't good at all. It tasted like a bunch of odds and ends mixed up together. It tasted like chicken soup with seafood in it.

"He was accustomed to cooking fried chicken," Woo said laughing out loud.

"Uh huh. He wanted pig in that gumbo."

"Yeah, Girl. That's probably what he and his mom were fighting about. His mama was asking, 'Where's the Pig, Bitch?" We both started laughing so hard.

After dinner, we watched the countdown to the New Year on television.

Thomas asked, "How did you like the gumbo?"

At first, I hesitant, but I felt I could be honest with him and that he wouldn't get offended.

I answered, "Thomas, it was good, but it wasn't gumbo. You have to remember, I go to New Orleans all of the time. So, I am used to having good gumbo."

He repeated, "It didn't taste like gumbo?"

"No, it was good, but it tasted like seafood soup."

He looked to be a little disappointed.

"Molly, maybe you should have said, 'Yes, it was very good, Thomas."

"Woo, I didn't wanna lie. His fat ass should learn how to cook it."

It's time to stop talking about that fucking gumbo, I thought as the clock ticked down—five, four, three, two, and one. HAPPY NEW YEAR!

The honking of the toy horns and the clanking of champagne flutes was sweet music to my hurting spirit. I drank punch with the two boys. Everybody else drank champagne. His mother and her fiancé were upstairs celebrating with the uncle. I thought it was a little rude, but I didn't say anything since I was a guest. Thomas tried his best to get me to drink alcohol, but I insisted on saying no to his invitation.

"Hmmm, he was trying to get you drunk. I wonder why?"

Woo asked, with a slight chuckle.

"That's not funny at all with your smart-ass!"

It seemed to be at that time a big relief from the pain of the previous year. I had made it through another holiday season. My New Year was coming in pretty damn good. I felt surrounded by what I perceived to be wonderful people. Thank God I didn't have to spend it by myself. It was a good celebration. This was a vastly different situation. It was wonderful, unique and pleasant. I forgot about the argument between Thomas and his mother. I didn't ask him anything about it. After we brought in the New Year, I waited about ten minutes, then went home. I didn't take any leftovers with me for obvious reasons.

"Molly, I've never known you to eat at other folks' houses," Woo said. "So, when did you start this?" she asked.

"I don't," I said hurriedly and shamefully.

The next day, Thomas called. He asked me to come over to his shop. I wasn't doing anything at the time, so I put on some clothes and drove out to his shop. When I arrived, I went inside and sat down. I watched as Britney and Tracey did repairs on a couple of chairs.

Thomas said, "I'm going to start training them on how to write grant proposals and solicit investors. Would you like to watch?" he asked.

I wanted to critique them as well. I thought it would be fun to act like a CEO, so I agreed.

"You trusted him to train them how to write? Did he train them to repair those damn chairs?" Woo asked tauntingly.

"Huh?" I asked.

"You heard me!"

Britney and Tracey went to get some food. That's when Thomas decided to present me with the contract. He charged a fee to write the proposal for the agency and to get investors. I took a look at it.

I said, "Come by the house later. So, we can talk more in detail."

I couldn't understand certain parts of the contract because it was mostly legal jargon.

He said, "OK, I don't have a problem with that."

I said, "I'm getting ready to leave. My head is killing me."

I gave him a check for four hundred dollars, which was for the first part of the EEOC. As I gathered my belongings to leave, Thomas presented a contract which stated that it would take twelve thousand dollars to start up the production of my modeling agency.

I said, "No way. I don't have money like that!"

"Well, we can crunch the numbers a little. So, what can you come up with?" he asked.

I said, "We'll talk later about this contract and the money."

Thomas called me the next day.

He said, "I wanna stop by and talk to you about the modeling agency. It's not out of my way."

"I'm a little bit tired. Can't we do this later in the week?" I asked.

Thomas said, "If you're gonna do the agency, then you should. If not, I have other things to do."

Damn, he sure is pressuring me; if I don't do it, he might steal my idea, I thought to myself.

I was so confused. I knew the modeling agency could turn into something big. All I needed was a photographer, along with someone to write the proposals for the grant money. This would have been the point where Thomas came into the picture.

Woo chuckled, "Dag, he had you fooled for real."

"What do you mean?"

"Mmmm, he took advantage of you. He knew you suffered from depression from your previous EEOC," Woo seemed disturbed.

He came by within the hour. We sat down and discussed the contract. I asked him about the 45% profit share that he wanted.

He said, "Well, I am going to be doing most of the work. Forty-five percent is not even half."

"Molly, if he got 45%, was he paying any expenses out of it?" Woo asked.

"Naw, I was responsible for all the expenses."

By this time a puzzled look crossed my face that only I could see. I knew where Woo was headed.

"You shoulda never let that fat son of a bitch in your house," Woo said in a measured tone.

"Woo, please be quiet so I can finish!"

I said, "Thomas, the first thing we need to do is go to an attorney and get the agency incorporated."

He said, "We'll do that in a couple of days."

"Will seven thousand get this started?"

"Yes," he said.

I just knew we could make this happen. I was so excited. I felt like a child at Christmas. I went on and signed the contract. I, then, gave him a check for seven thousand dollars. We both had original copies of the agreement.

"Well, I'm not going to stay. I have a lot of work cut out for me. Between my upholstery shop and your agency, I need to get started."

"Ok, so, I'll call you tomorrow," I said.

After he left, I started calling all my acquaintances to tell them about this new adventure. I called friends who had successful businesses. I asked them to invest until I got the grant money. I explained that they would be reimbursed once I got the grant money. The next day, I had two verbal commitments. They totaled thirty six hundred dollars. I had also gotten verbal commitments from twelve models. Everybody was excited. The only thing the models needed was a release paper to take to their photographer. My friends needed a contract with the agency's name on it. They were not handing me checks without legitimate agreements. I picked up the phone and called Thomas.

I asked, "When are we supposed to be going to the attorney to get incorporated?"

He said, "Well, they're busy, but I'll get Britney to make an appointment this week."

"I'm probably gonna have to find Ms. Chocolate so that she can do that Ice Burg shoot. Her regular dance club caught on fire last week."

Thomas asked, "How did it catch on fire?"

I answered, "This goes on all the time in the strip club industry. Do you remember that time when this guy named Marlon was accused of burning down Magic?"

He said, "Not really."

I went on to tell him the story about Marlon being accused of hiring someone to break the Mayor legs. I told him that I heard about it on the news.

He said, "Well, I heard Mr. Cortez say on his radio show one day that the mayor was actually gay."

I said, "It was mentioned during the mayor's trial that a man named Luey was living in his basement for years without paying any rent."

We also discussed the two women who had kicked my ass

in the hallway of my condominium building. By this time, the conversation had gone way off on a tangent onto subjects that had nothing to do with the tasks that we had united to accomplish. I didn't know it at the time, but the implications of the subject matter would be used against me in an extremely improbable fashion.

"Girl, I've worked at the Gentleman's club. So, you know I know 'bout that industry. Hell, that's where I met you," Woo stated.

"Yup, I remember meeting your fine ass. Things really worked out for the best. Even though, I did wanna hit that back then," I joked.

"Nah, you know I don't swing that way. I wish I coulda been with you that night though, I woulda kicked them bitches' asses!" Woo said, raising her voice in mock anger.

"I'm about to get to the part 'bout that bitch ass Thomas. It's gonna trip you out," I said.

By this time, we had been conversing for nearly nine hours. I was talking and Woo was mainly listening.

After this conversation, of part pertinent talk and part gossip, I told Thomas in an excited voice about my progress in getting investors for the agency.

"Guess what, Thomas? I got two investors today. They're willing to commit to thirty-six hundred dollars already!" I said.

"Wow! That was quick. How did you manage that?" Thomas asked.

"Remember, I told you that my dentist friend and my friend who owns a rim shop were gonna invest?"

"Your doctor friend should be investing in my elite upholstery shop," Thomas stated flatly.

"Why you say that? What does a furniture store have to do

with a modeling agency?" I asked, with a part questioning and part pissed-off look on my face.

"Well, he's a DOCTOR. I need investors for my furniture shop. You know I just started it," he said. I imagined him rolling his eyes.

"I have a concern about the models. Some of them may be strippers. I don't feel comfortable having them coming in and out of my shop," Thomas said sounding like a sissy.

"So, what do you propose we do about that?" I asked.

"You could rent the office next door for the photo shoots. It would only cost eight hundred dollars a month."

"No, the agreement was to do the photo shoots in the back of your shop. We'll just stick to that," I objected.

"Okay then. Now, back to your doctor friend. I think he should consider investing in my shop since it's already established. When we get the grant money coming in for the agency, I'll give you back 20% of the profit share," Thomas said.

I quickly cut him off.

I said, "I did mention your furniture shop, but he only wants to invest in my modeling agency."

I didn't mention shit, but I had to shut his fat ass up. Why would he even think that someone would want to invest in a damn furniture shop? This is when a major red flag went up in my head. At this point, I knew that even though the contract stated that Thomas's obligations were to get investors for the agency within four weeks, his true agenda was to secure investors for his furniture shop. I knew when Thomas made that statement; he was only thinking about investors for his shop. He couldn't give a rat's ass about my welfare. I attempted to call him the next day, but he was too busy to speak with me. I called back later to his cell phone and he wouldn't answer.

He had turned his cell phone off. The very next day, the same thing happened again. After this nonsense, I called his shop. Britney answered the phone. I insisted on speaking to Thomas. She gave him the phone. His fat ass had all kinds of excuses as to why he neither answered nor returned my calls. Less than a minute into our conversation, he said, "I'll call you 'rat' back in about an hour." He was trying to say right back. Well, the "rat" had a long ass tail. Hours passed with no call from Thomas. I called him and called him until I finally reach him at two in the damn morning. He tried to sound like he was so groggy and completely out of it.

"Thomas, this is Molly. I've been calling you all day."

"Molly, you have to understand my medical condition. I have Vertigo and I stay tired a lot. I don't know why my black clients think they can just call me any time of the night and this time of morning," he said insultingly in his half-sleepy drone.

"Thomas, you were calling me at two in the morning just days ago, but it was ok then. Now, it's a problem?"

"Don't call me, at NO two in the morning!" He shouted.

"You don't have to worry 'bout me calling you this early anymore, but if I can't reach you during the day, what are my options?" I asked. "Thomas, if you treat your black clients this way, I see why there's a problem. I'm sure you answer and return your white clients' calls," I said defiantly, feeling very insulted by the implication that, it was I, and not him, who was being unprofessional and unreasonable.

Thomas wanted to argue.

I said, "I'm coming by your office to see the progress report on the grant proposals."

Allegedly, he had spent three days working on it. He claimed he paid Britney and some of her friends to write up the proposals. The next day, I couldn't get to him on the phone. I called him once more. This time, he answered.

"Thomas, I need all my receipts!"

"First of all, I gave the graphics design firm a check for twenty two hundred dollars to begin the project. Then I had to pay Britney and her friends' cash for their work," he said, in a tone, suggesting that I had no reason to question the veracity of his statements.

I looked at the telephone receiver with a wide-eyed stare which mimicked one of his best saucer-eyed looks.

"You mean to tell me you paid someone in cash!"

"Yes," he responded.

"Thomas, why in the world would you pay somebody in cash? You need to get Britney to go back to each one of her friends that she paid or you paid and get me receipts. By the way, how much cash are we speaking of?" I said forcefully.

"It was three hundred dollars," he said, still using the superior and defiant tone.

"I need receipts, Thomas. You know that anytime you have a business, you always get receipts, if for no other reason than for records and tax purposes. You should know this, Thomas," I demanded.

"Well, it's Phyllis's birthday and I'm grieving. Can we just do this some other day?" he asked, with a sound of hurt that could have been real, but also could have been easily faked.

"What are you telling your white clients when they walk into your shop or call you? So you're telling them you're grieving? Thomas, I grieve every day over my mother. Another thing, how can you be grieving so hard when you said last week that you're gonna marry some African woman?" I asked.

I was looking through the telephone receiver as if I could see him. My eyes were like lasers traveling over the phone lines, burning a hole in his fat ass head.

"I'm sure Phyllis would want me to be happy," he said sounding much like he was a soap opera character.

"Well, I'm getting dressed as we speak. I'll be there in a couple of hours."

At that point, I hung up. Barely five minutes later, I received an email. It read:

Britney has the receipts you requested. I spoke with my photographer today. We're both excited about the modeling agency. He's excited to work with the girls. We came up with a name for your agency. I'll be printing the business cards on tomorrow.

This is when I decided to call him. He answered.

"Hello, Thomas. I read your email. I'm interested in knowing the name that you and your photographer came up with?"

Unless the name was a vast improvement over Ten Cents, it was a moot point.

"We came up with a great name! The Alley," Thomas said with an enthusiasm that seemed insincere.

"The Alley is the name of a European modeling agency! Didn't you know that? What happened to the name I came up with?" I asked defiantly.

"Well, I checked with the secretary of state and the office said that the name, The Alley, was available," he responded.

"Thomas, this is why we need an attorney. The Alley is already taken. The Alley is probably under an umbrella of other businesses," I shot back.

Thomas was silent, but only for a moment. He knew that he had made a mistake. I also asked him about the business cards.

"Thomas, how can you print up business cards without first speaking to an attorney? You should know how important it is to get incorporated. This was the first thing we were gonna do. What's the damn problem? If you had printed the cards using the name The Alley, you woulda had to throw all those cards away," I fumed.

He was silent and I was fed up at this point.

"You know, Thomas, you've gone back on your word more than once. You've tried to rename MY modeling agency. First, it was The Modeling Shop, then The Alley. You claimed you didn't have receipts. Then, you e-mail me five minutes later saying that you have them. Where did they come from so fast?" I asked. "Also, when I call, you don't answer. When you do answer, you're either busy or grieving or so you say. Then, you wanna argue with me just because I asked you for my receipts, which I am entitled to. So at this point, I think you should just give me all my money back and we end this association!" I said in a demanding tone.

"You and Maggie are just alike. Let me call you back. I have to step out for a couple of hours."

"Naw, damn it. You can leave Maggie out of this. You need to give me my money back, Thomas!"

That asshole hung up the phone on me. I called him right back and he picked up.

I immediately said, "This is not like you and Maggie. Don't you ever compare me to her again. We're talking 'bout seven thousand dollars! This is serious. Some people call it blood money!"

Thomas became very quiet for about ten seconds. At that point, he began to defend himself.

"What about all the materials that I've researched for your agency? What about the money I've paid to people?" He asked.

"You said that you were gonna hire a market research

team. Supposedly, it was the same market research team that did work for "The Apprentice". So, what happened to them? Thomas, I want my money back 'cause you're playing games."

I had gotten tired of Thomas's shit.

"You're just like Maggie!" he said once more and this made my blood boil.

"Didn't I tell you not to ever compare me to your and Maggie's ordeal? This is BLOOD MONEY, Thomas! I'm gonna call everybody in your area and tell them about what happened to me with this money deal. Thomas, I'm also gonna call the Valletta Chamber of Commerce!" I shouted.

He became very hostile, said a few choice words, and then hung up. I went straight to my computer. I did an internet search for the graphics company that he claimed he had paid the twenty- two hundred dollars to. I found them.

"Molly, he sounds like he was just trying to twist shit around. Hell, he went back on his word and tried to say that you did," Woo chuckled.

"Wait up, girl. Listen to this!"

I called the graphic design firm. A young man by the name of Rodney answered. He was gonna put together a web page for the agency, complete with flyers, calendars and business cards. I told him who I was.

I asked, "Did Thomas give you any money to do work for my modeling agency?"

Rodney responded, "Thomas gave us a twenty two hundred dollar check. It had your name on the memo line, but we credited it toward his past due account of twenty two hundred dollars. We can never start up a new project if there's an outstanding balance on another account."

I told him about my situation.

Rodney said, "Hold on. I'm gonna call Thomas on three way."

During the conversation, Thomas said, "Rodney, don't worry because I'm on the phone with the District Attorney's office as we speak. Just go ahead and credit my account. I'll pay Molly back out of my own personal account."

Thomas hung up.

Rodney clicked over and said to me, "Well, I hope everything works out for you."

However, the tone of his voice had a ring of doubt.

****

"Damn, this is some real trippin shit! That bitch done stole your money AND your modeling agency idea! That bitch ain't shit. He ain't nothing but a con artist. He was up to no good from the start!" Woo screamed over the phone.

"You ain't heard nothing yet, wait till I tell you 'bout the murder," I lamented.

"What murder? You keep saying it. So, when you gonna talk about it? Damn!"

"Hold your horses, Woo. I'm getting to that part."

Within three days of my conversation with Rodney, I received six e-mails from Thomas. He said that I had threatened him and that he was afraid for his family's life. In the e-mails, he claimed that I was in a gang which involved burning down buildings and breaking people's legs and hiding in bushes waiting to beat people up. The letters were so well constructed. If someone had read them, they would have believed every word Thomas wrote. He cleverly used our previous conversations against me. He had twisted my statements to create the worst lies that I had ever heard in my life.

At this point, I'm wondering who or what in the hell was I dealing with. This man was a tremendous con artist. I asked God, How could this happen to me again? What is Thomas planning to do? I had fasted over my decision before I finally decided to sign the contract with him. There were no signs. However, there were clear signs that I ignored. The red flags were flying high during the New Year's Eve celebration with Thomas and his family. In looking back, God was telling me what to do, but I wasn't paying close enough attention. I wanted what I wanted. I wanted to believe in what I was doing. My mistake was putting my trust in Thomas. Or maybe my mistake was I had been serving two masters.

"What does that mean?" Woo asked.

"I'll get to that," I said.

I began to enter into the worst state of depression over my misstep with Thomas. It was a feeling that overloaded my entire soul. It spilled over into my physical world. I could barely walk. My voice became weak and my face became frail. I wondered if God had forsaken me. I kept calling out to Him asking, God, please give me strength. He had always been there for me in the past, despite my transgressions. I couldn't let this debacle stop me. I couldn't let Thomas get away with his thievery.

"I'm glad you didn't let this bad experience turn you away from God," Woo said in a soft tone.

"Yeah, some folk turn away and never look back!" I stated.

"I know a few that had one bad experience and they stopped believing."

"Woo, keep in mind, at this point, I didn't know nothing 'bout a murder."

"What murder? Damn it."

"Trust me. I'm gonna tell you, girl."

Finally, a couple days later, my strength began to come back. I decided to file a theft by deception warrant against Thomas. It was theft and it was deception. At the time, I couldn't think of any one better to call on than an old familiar lawyer named Mike. He caught my attention while I was in court. He had on a silk suit. He had a unique style about him. Mike was so suave. I asked Mike for a business card. I had to get him to go to court with me. This case involved ten thousand dollars. It was also theft by deception. It took a year for me to get my money back, but I did. So, I called Mike and made an appointment. When I arrived at his office, he still looked like the Mike that I had met years ago. He just had a few hairs missing on the tip of his head. I told him about my situation with Thomas. As I concluded, he rolled his eyes.

"Molly, why is this kind of stuff always happening to you with these men?" Mike asked.

"Stuff. What do you mean by stuff?"

"Last time, it was a guy, as I recall, ripping you off. Now, this fellow."

"Mike, the previous theft by deception case was a business deal that had no relationship with this one. So, let's get this straight! My situation with this man is a business deal with totally different aspects. So, don't get it twisted. Hell, I've had bad experiences with females, too," I said.

I got him back on the right path real quick.

Mike requested that I give him six hundred dollars as a retainer. He said, "In the meantime, I'm gonna try to get your money back without having to go to court."

I said, "It would be great if you could manage to do that."

"Do you have the graphic designer's phone number?"

"Yeah, I do!"

He called him while I was in his office. He put the speakerphone on for me to hear.

Rodney said, "Thomas gave us twenty-two hundred dollars, but it was credited toward his past due account for the same amount."

Mike asked Rodney to send him an e-mail with all of the information that he had just quoted to him. The information arrived within minutes. At that point, I wrote Mike a check for six hundred dollars.

I said to him while endorsing the check, "Now, Mike, you gonna show up for court, right?"

"Yes. Do I need to give you a contract?"

"No, dude. I trust you!"

We both laughed as I left his office.

The days were long. The nights were sleepless. I couldn't help but to think about the entire ordeal. How did I let this happen to me again? At night, I rehashed my business deal with Thomas over and over. I repeated word for word all of our conversations. I thought about the meeting that we had at the shop with Britney and Tracey. I thought about the New Year's Eve celebration at his mother's house. I concluded that it was all orchestrated. Yes, Thomas had planned out this entire con game to the smallest detail. Thomas had never even thought about a modeling agency. Hell, he never thought about investors! He researched the viability of it by going online. He used images of different models without them physically being present and without their permission for the shoots. Thomas basically typed out information about the models to coincide with their pictures. This simple process took literally ten minutes.

Thomas knew that I suffered from depression. He thought he could get the best of me. He thought that I would just go away. He was oh so wrong! The case was finally scheduled for court. In the meantime, I couldn't get this shit off my mind. It was in my dreams! I carried it with me throughout the day. I was constantly thinking about it and talking about it with anyone who listened. One night, I was awakened around two in the morning by an image that looked like a thin black woman. I was shaking like hell. I was so scared! In my dazed condition, I wasn't totally awake but I could hear the apparition say, "Ask Maggie about Thomas's first wife." Then the spirit faded away.

"Molly, what's up with this Maggie chick? Why was she such a friend to this obviously crooked bastard?" Woo asked in a loud tone.

"I started feeling the same way, Woo!"

I didn't forget about what Thomas had told me the week before I signed the contract. He told me that Barry's mother had passed away some years ago. I remembered asking him about getting married to the African woman. His ensuing response was, "It depends on whether or not it's worth it." I just sat there in bed thinking about what I had seen and heard that day. I had so many pressing questions concerning Thomas. I wanted to call Maggie right then. I decided, however to wait until the next day. I called Maggie around noon.

I asked, "What happened to Thomas's first wife?"

Her revelation blew me away. It was incredible! At first, I thought Maggie was just kidding with me. She can be a bigtime jokester at times. She assured me that her story was one hundred percent true.

Maggie said, "Thomas told me that Barry was a product of a rape. It occurred while Barry's mother was in college. It was a white college professor that raped her. After Barry's mom made the allegation, she had to leave the college. Supposedly, the administration made things so hard for her that she was forced out. While she was pregnant, she met and fell in love with Thomas. They eventually married. Months after they exchanged vows, Thomas buried his wife. He raised Barry as his own son."

Now, this story was in complete opposition to what Thomas had told me. He told me that both of his son's mothers were deceased. He said that Barry got his gray eyes from his grandmother's side of the family. He didn't mention anything about Barry's mom being pregnant when he met her. Nor did he mention that Barry was a product of rape. Maggie went on to drop the second bombshell!

"Molly, you wanna know what happened to Phyllis?" she asked, with a serious, cryptic tone to her voice.

"I already know. She died from issues dealing with the post office."

"Nope. Thomas killed her," she said without as much as a pause.

"Maggie, I'm not in the mood for any games. How did he kill Phyllis?" I asked, with a strong tone of skepticism in my voice.

Maggie said that she went over to Thomas's home right after Phyllis's death to show her sympathy. She went to hug Thomas. He turned away from her and said, "I've been smoking."

I asked, "Smoking what, Marijuana?"

"I don't know so I can't comment," Maggie waffled.

"Don't you know what marijuana smells like?"

"No, I never tried it."

"Hell, you've been around people that smoke it. I'm sure."

"No I haven't," Maggie said angrily.

"Bullshit, Maggie! You expect me to believe that? By the way, your friend Thomas cheated me out of seven thousand dollars!"

"You can believe what you want."

"So, you guys been talking?" I asked.

"We spoke for just a minute. That's all."

"Maggie, just finish telling me what you and Thomas talked about since he wouldn't let you hug him." I said with disgust.

Maggie said she found that comment to be strange because she never knew Thomas to be a smoker. So, she ignored it. Thomas intimated that he had changed Phyllis's medicine.

Maggie said that Thomas said, "Phyllis kept screaming out in pain, so I gave her 800 milligrams of Ibuprofen every two hours, just to shut her up. That's when Phyllis began foaming at the mouth. Mucus was coming out of her nose, but I didn't think anything of it."

Maggie began to really shoot off at the mouth. She said on several occasions that Thomas would say terrible things about Phyllis to her. She said that she heard Thomas's mother telling him to get rid of Phyllis.

His mother said, "She's too sickly and she's just holding you back, Thomas."

Maggie even witnessed an argument between Thomas and Phyllis.

"Thomas slammed the phone down. Afterwards he kept saying, 'I wish she was dead! I wish she would go ahead and die!' He kept saying it over and over," Maggie said.

This shocking account left me speechless, but only for a moment.

"Maggie, you didn't tell me this story when I was questioning you 'bout whether or not I should go into business with him!"

"What do you mean?" Maggie asked.

"You more or less said that he would make a good business partner."

"Molly, I wasn't thinking about all of this at that time."

"Maggie, how in the hell could you forget about what you just told me? If I had been in your place, I would have called the fucking police."

"I'm sorry."

"Maggie, if I had known all this shit, there's no way I woulda gone into business with Thomas! Why didn't you tell me this?"

I was livid as anyone would be after such a confession.

"I didn't think Thomas was serious about wanting her dead," Maggie said.

I sat for a second and thought how much of a dumb ass that she must be, trying to act so naïve and innocent.

"Maggie, what about the 800 milligrams of Ibuprofen? That much medicine once every two hours means that in eight hours he had given her 3200 milligrams. That's over 12,000 milligrams in a day. That's more than overdosing. A person with a third grade education can read the label and know that the level of dosage is 400 milligrams every six hours," I said forcefully.

"I just didn't know what to think," she said as though that simple answer would suffice.

"At least you could have told me," I pleaded.

At that moment I had a feeling that came over me and I knew that it was the spirit of Phyllis. I could in fact feel her presence. I had been seeing apparitions over the past few weeks of a black woman with a white gown. This is why I always sleep with a light on. Now, I knew that it was Phyllis. Yup, it was Phyllis. She was coming to me, prodding for me to find out the truth about what really happened to her.

"Molly, I never knew why you kept a light on. I figured that you were scared of the dark, but I didn't think that it was that serious," Woo said.

"Yup, it's a scary thing, although they don't try to hurt me. They just scare the piss out of me. That's all," I chuckled.

"That Maggie sounds like a really weak bitch!" Woo stated.

"Yup, she's full of shit if she claims that she didn't suspect something."

"Hold up! Hold up! Wait a damn minute here!" Woo screamed, "Didn't Thomas tell you that his own mother was raped in college by a white professor?"

"Dang! He sure did. He's a lying sick bitch."

That following weekend, I began an internet search on that wretched unknown and yet to be convicted criminal. Thomas had literally gotten away with murder. I went from web site to web site trying to come up with information on Thomas. I finally found a web site called "Net Detectives." I found information on Thomas and his entire family, with the exception of his father. I also found Phyllis's brother's telephone number and address. It took a lot of nerve for me to call her brother.

Thomas had mentioned to me that he and Phyllis's family were not speaking anymore for some reason. At that point, I began to pray over making the phone call to Phyllis's brother. I asked God to guide and direct me. I didn't want to call him and get hung up on. I basically didn't want to get my feelings hurt. I found out through Net Detectives that Thomas was married before to a woman named Bernice Walters. I found Bernice's address and phone number. I mustered enough courage to call the two numbers the website listed. Both numbers were to a homeless shelter in Chicago. Thomas and his entire family migrated from Chicago. When I called the first shelter which was within a hospital, I found a trail of information. I found out from the first shelter that Bernice was only forty-four years old.

The clerk at the shelter said, "Oh yeah. You talking about light-skinned Nicee."

I said, "Yup," hoping to get more information.

He said, "I haven't seen her in two years, but, yeah, she used to be a nurse here. Are you a family member?"

"Yes. Can you have her to call this number if you see her?"

He took down my number. I also tried to sneak in a question about Thomas.

"Did you know her husband, Thomas?"

He said quickly, "I don't know nothing about a husband. I'll give her this information. I've told you too much already and we're not supposed to give out any information."

I thanked him for his help and we hung up.

I also tried to call back at different times to the shelter. I tried to get a different person on the phone. I couldn't get anybody to give me any information. Bernice obviously didn't want to be found. Then it dawned on me why the man at the shelter put so much emphasis on light skin. Bernice must have been extremely light-skinned. She must have looked almost white. All of the evidence was now adding up. Thomas's oldest son wasn't from a rape in college. Chances are no damn body was ever raped in college. This was indeed Barry's mother and she's not dead. A question formed in the back of my mind. Why doesn't she have her son? The ultra-light-skinned Bernice is still alive! I wonder if Barry knows that his mother is still alive.

"Molly, I think Thomas told him that his mother was dead!" Woo said angrily.

"Woo, you're probably right."

Why would Thomas keep Bernice such a secret? Why would a woman who is forty-four years old and a nurse be living in homeless shelters? I said to myself.

All the pieces were starting to fit together into a puzzle that still made little sense. I also found out through Net Detectives that Phyllis's home was in Thomas's uncle's name. Thomas managed to convince Phyllis to sell her old home in South Georgia. He probably used the proceeds from the sale to put toward the home that he purchased using the uncle's name. I found that even his mother's home was in his uncle's and mother's fiancé's name.

"What the hell is up with this fucked-up family? You would make a damn good detective!" Woo stated.

Maggie also mentioned to me that Thomas had met Phyllis over the internet. He told Phyllis that he wasn't moving to Georgia until she married him. According to Net Detectives, Phyllis went to Chicago to be with him. Phyllis got pregnant with Little T. Thomas married her. He then moved to Georgia and brought his entire family. During that time, Thomas got a position with the postal service as a temporary employee. He somehow managed to finagle a detail into the EEOC department. This kind of rapid movement is unheard of. This branch of the government possesses very personal files involving private medical histories of individuals throughout the United States.

How in the hell did Thomas manage this? Until this day, the government inspectors have made it a secret as to the ruse that he used to ascend so quickly into the ranks of such an important organization. I then contacted a close friend of mine in the personnel department. I asked him to check and see how long Thomas worked for the government. I gave him all of the names that I came up with through Net Detectives. He put me on hold for about eight or so minutes, then he came back to the phone.

He said, "I can't find him in the system."

"Are you positive?"

"I did a twenty year search. No one by either name could be found to match his demographics."

I asked my friend to check Phyllis's records. He found Phyllis easily.

"Who does Phyllis have listed as her spouse or beneficiary?"

He said, "Phyllis doesn't have anyone listed as dependants nor as a beneficiary."

I went on from there to call the supervisor of timekeepers. I asked for the manager. Marilyn came to the phone. I told her what had happened with the seven thousand dollars and what I now suspected Thomas of. She looked into the system files.

She stated, "No one by that name ever worked for the postal service!"

I responded, "Marilyn, there must be a mistake!"

She said, "No, the system would pull it up if he ever worked in this district."

I asked Marilyn if she would call down to the EEOC department and ask about Thomas because I knew for a fact that he had worked under Ms. Jiles. She agreed to call. She said to me, "I'll get back to you with the results of the conversation."

I waited twenty minutes. I called Marilyn back. She said, "I called down to EEOC, but no one knew of or had heard of a Thomas."

I thought that they would have told her the truth since she was a manager. When I called EEOC, they quickly told me they couldn't give out any information on persons who previously had worked there. Now, I knew Thomas had worked for the postal service because Maggie worked with him in the computer room before Thomas got detailed to EEOC.

What happened in the EEOC department with Thomas? I thought about what Thomas said. He told me that management harassed Ms. Jiles so bad that she had a nervous breakdown. I did remember seeing Ms. Jiles several times in the cafeteria. She looked as if she had a nervous problem. Ms. Jiles's unsightly appearance was so noticeable because she once was a very beautiful female. She could now be seen sitting in the cafeteria alone and despondent. She had gained so much weight. It was obvious to me that something drastic had happened to her. I wondered if whatever happened to her, happened while Thomas was working with her. Thomas may have stolen records and all the blame came back to Ms. Jiles. The end result was Ms. Jiles was demoted and harassed until she had a nervous breakdown. Whether or not Thomas was the central culprit in all of this may never be known.

Thomas told me that Phyllis had a lawsuit against the postal service because the supervisor had hit her. I had my suspicion that Thomas was feeding me bullshit! His existence within the government was a lie. Apparently, he had used an alias name. No records could substantiate him ever being employed at the postal service. The evidence I had uncovered pointed to Thomas stealing files of cases that had been won to assist with his filings of Phyllis's case.

Woo shouted, "Like I said before, that bitch-ass sissy was lying 'bout being Jewish, and he was just a big ass liar period. Shit, this phone is beginning to burn my right ear! Hold for a sec. I gotta switch ears before my ear cooks off! Let me put this phone on this charger 'cause I'm not waiting till tomorrow to hear the rest of this unbelievable shit!"

"I told you, it was unbelievable," I said.

"Hurry up and get to the damn murder part!" Woo shouted.

"I am at the murder part, but let me finish tell you this part."

At that point I decided to call the County hospital to see why they didn't investigate Phyllis's death. I also called the District Attorney's office and the County Examiner's office. I wanted to know the protocol for patients brought in for what seemed to be a case of drug overdose. They all said, "If the doctors thought anything was suspicious then they would contact the medical examiner's office." At that point, I contacted the medical examiner's office. At first he couldn't pull up a Phyllis Walters; it was on a Friday afternoon so he wanted to order the death certificate and get back with me on the following Monday.

That weekend, I managed to reach Maggie. I said to her, "I get the impression from the medical examiner that Phyllis didn't die in the county she lived."

"Really," she responded.

I was really in shock over finding this out and so was she, at least she sounded surprised. Monday morning finally came and I received a call from the medical examiner's assistant. She said, "Phyllis Walters did in fact die at the local medical hospital." I was unknowingly spelling her name wrong. I found out that Phyllis's first name was in fact spelled Phillis instead of Phyllis.

Obviously, the doctors didn't suspect foul play, that's why they didn't do an investigation, I thought.

The assistant said to me, 'There's no way for the county to initiate an investigation since there's no body to examine." She continued, "The family would have to hire an attorney to get the medical records, and then go to the District Attorney's office with sufficient evidence."

I thought to myself, even with the facts at hand there was enough evidence for negligence. None of these people at the medical examiner's office were seriously considering what I was saying. I only imagined what families have gone through with DA's and medical examiners and police detectives, when it comes to their suspicions of a loved one being murdered by a husband or wife. Maybe this inaction is why, in many cases, there's a second murder committed before the perpetrator gets caught. Now I knew, I had to put together enough faith and courage and strength to call Phyllis's brother and I did. I called her brother and, lo and behold, he answered the phone. I immediately identified myself. I quickly went on to say that I knew Thomas Walters and that I was involved in a legal issue with him.

I said, "I'm so sorry to hear about Phyllis's death." I said all of this to him in what felt like one breath. He was quiet and I was nervous as hell. I went on to say, "I've been having many sleepless nights. I prayed that you would at least be open minded enough to listen to me." I made it clear that this had nothing to do with any vengeance toward Thomas.

He reassured me by saying, "OK, I'm listening."

I went detail by detail from the business arrangement with Thomas to my conversations with Maggie. I told him every thing Maggie said to me. Maggie's exact words.

After listening to me, he said, "That's a lot for me take in."

I got a few questions in.

I asked, "Did you know that Thomas was married before he married Phyllis?"

He answered, "No."

I mentioned to him that I tried to find Thomas in the personnel system of the postal service. He could not be found. The brother found that to be strange, because to his knowledge Thomas did in fact work for the EEOC as a temporary employee.

I asked, "Did the immediate family request to have Phyllis cremated?"

He said quickly, "No! Thomas went and had that done without our consent, we were very upset because we wanted to have a burial for Phyllis." He then asked for my number and said, "I'm gonna call my brother and if we decided to pursue the issue, we'll call you back."

I replied, "I think that you all should look into this because something's not right here. Sir, please don't think that I'm trying to get back at Thomas. This has really been bothering my heart. I truly believe that he deliberately killed your sister. Did you know that Phyllis received a settlement from the postal service back in December or January for sixty-eight thousand dollars?"

He became quiet as if he didn't know.

He responded, "We'll call you back later in the week."

We hung up.

Days went by and no call. I'm thinking, he's not gonna call back. Damn! Thomas is gonna get away with murder! I have to admit that I was only 95% sure Thomas killed his wife. Finally, I got a call from both brothers and one of their wives. I had to sit up and be strong. I told them the story just as I had explained it to Maggie. These individuals were very articulate. So, I had to be also.

I only imagined how sweet of a person Phyllis was. I imagined her to be strong minded, but someone who unknowingly got caught up with the devil's co-worker. The apparition that came to me, though hazy, was tall and gaunt. She looked sad.

I truly believed Phyllis could have lived longer. I've known people who had suffered from different debilitating diseases, yet they had managed to live productive lives. Those people couldn't have any stress in their lives, though. Thomas and his family had created a great deal of stress for Phyllis, deliberately. According to her brother, Thomas knew of Phyllis's illness through their correspondences via email. He admitted to Phyllis's brother that he was only marrying Phyllis for her employment benefits. He told Phyllis exactly what Thomas had admitted. The saga was beginning to come together, yet the logic of it all still made little sense to me.

"Did he really admit that to you, knowing you were gonna tell her?" I asked.

"Yes! At that point, we pretty much started to suspect that his intentions were not good for my sister. We practically begged Phyllis several times to leave that stressful situation," the brother stated.

"Did you know Thomas filed for a divorce? I think that you should check into her beneficiary money from the postal service. Phyllis didn't have Thomas down as a beneficiary, nor was Little T. I know that Thomas is trying very hard to get this money, but he can't," I explained.

Phyllis's sister-in-law was in agreement with me. She wanted Phyllis's death to be investigated.

She said, "Thomas was rarely at the hospital during the time Phyllis was admitted. He was away taking care of his shop, as though Phyllis was no more than an afterthought."

According to the brother, the doctor who attended to Phyllis asked Thomas why he didn't bring her in sooner.

Thomas told the doctor, "I didn't know Phyllis was giving herself all that medication."

The brother stated that the doctor seemed curious since the

circumstances were suspicious. He kept asking questions, but Thomas kept giving him answers which explained each question. I can only imagine what he was saying with his forked serpent of a tongue as he pretended to be so distraught.

The brother said that the doctor stated, "Phyllis had the worst case of renal failure that I've ever observed during my medical career or even heard or read of!"

"Was she on dialysis?" Woo asked.

"No! This is why she could have been saved," I explained.

"Molly, I'm surprised the brother didn't hang up on you the first time you called."

I had prayed about it before I made that call. All of the relatives stated that when Phyllis died, Thomas showed absolutely no remorse. He acted quickly to have Phyllis's body cremated. It was now clear that this was done to eliminate any physical evidence of him purposefully overdosing her. He wanted there to be nothing used or tested that could possibly convict him of wrongdoing.

The sister-in-law was on my side concerning Thomas. Our strong belief was that he intentionally hurt Phyllis. She wanted to move forward toward justice. The brothers were beginning to become a little reluctant. They were not quite as accepting of pursuing justice as they were in the beginning. I felt as though the brothers feared Thomas and his possible retaliation. Something must have happened in the past seven years which the family was not revealing. There was no way a family would just let a revelation like this simply be swept neatly away underneath a rug of deceit without investigating the allegation, especially if they felt there was foul play involved. It was obvious Thomas had put fear into Phyllis's family.

Before we ended the conversation, I told them that is was

now up to them to proceed. I had done what Phyllis had prodded me to do, which was to reveal the truth to them. I had basically done all the homework for them. I found out things that they probably would never have known otherwise. I can only hope that the spirit of Phyllis can find some peace.

Woo asked, "Didn't you say earlier that Thomas and Phyllis had gotten a settlement from the postal service?"

"Yeah, Phyllis had gotten a settlement from her EEOC case three weeks prior to her death. So, Thomas couldn't say that he didn't have the money for her final expenses," I responded.

According to the sister-in-law, after dealing with Thomas for seven years, they really didn't expect him to cry or show any emotion concerning Phyllis. The sister-in-law also said that their experiences with Thomas over those seven years were quite an ordeal. She said that he was a hard person to deal with. Now, I can only imagine the hell that he took her family through and the certain chaos that he caused Phyllis. I told them that I wasn't gonna mention what we had spoken about at the application hearing. They were happy to hear that. Phyllis's brothers were mostly concerned over Thomas not letting them spend any time with their nephew, Little T., especially if he knew that we were having such intimate conversation. They said that he would do something like not answer their calls or cut off communications completely. I told them that Thomas wasn't taking care of Little T. He was living at his grandmother's house.

I remember Thomas saying to Little T once when he had started to whine, "Stop it! Dry up those tears and be a man."

He said to stop it and be a man to a baby who was no more than seven years old. I thought that was a bit strong for a kid to interpret, especially right after dealing with his mother's death.

Our conversation had generally gone well. According to the detectives and the medical examiner's office, if they decided to pursue filing any charges against Thomas, they would have to retain an attorney. I also gave them the name of an attorney who I had met, who seemed to be an ideal choice for such a task facing them. Her name was Cathy. I had spoken to this attorney over the phone a day before my conversation with Phyllis's family. I felt as though she came across confident and strong. Cathy had a prior caseload, so she couldn't accommodate me. She made such an impression on me.

I was caught between a proverbial rock and a hard place with no attorney and little time. The attorney, whom I thought I had secured days before, Mike, did not return my calls to confirm our court appointment. Consequently, I had to take whomever I could get. Eventually, I met with an attorney named Jay. The meeting lasted thirty minutes. Jay had his son with him at the office. His son was a little hyperactive and he kept coming in the room every minute it seemed. However, I found Jay to be satisfactory. I gave him a check for five hundred dollars as a retainer.

Before the hearing, I was at home thinking back to the time I first met Thomas. I tried to put myself in his place to see how he viewed me during that time. Obviously, his perception of me was that I was weak. Thomas only saw me when I was severely depressed. He had yet to see the strong person that I can be when I had the time to marshal my forces. Thomas met me during the time that I was being harassed by my supervisor and simultaneously dealing with my mother's sickness and eventual death.

"Did Maggie's sorry ass go to court with you?" Woo asked.

"I asked her to go, but she claimed she had something to

do."

"Did she show up with Thomas? Was that her something to do?" Woo asked with a forceful tone.

"Woo, PLEASE let me finish."

"Go on, but this crooked-ass Maggie bitch is beginning to piss me off," Woo said out loud.

The day of the application hearing, I imagined that court would be a little difficult. I knew Thomas would be very convincing in front of the judge. I could just feel without even hearing one word of his testimony that he had convinced his attorney of his total innocence.

Woo stated, "I think Thomas told his attorney that he would give him some profit share once he got your modeling agency as an incentive. He seemed to be big on this profit share thing."

"I'm sure he did. He probably promised Maggie some, too," I said with a sad tone.

"What does Maggie look like Molly?" Woo asked.

"RUPAUL," I replied. We both laughed.

Even though I had retained Jay during my haste to scrounge up representation, I had left a voice message for an attorney by the name of Katherine. She sounded so competent and forceful over the voice message. She returned my call right away. We went into details about my case.

"Katherine, would you feel comfortable with another attorney appearing with you in court?"

"I can handle it myself. I don't need anybody appearing with me."

Jay's meek demeanor was overwhelmed by what I was hearing from Katherine. I was sure that Thomas would have strong and aggressive counsel. I couldn't afford to be represented by a milquetoast. I needed strength and confidence. So,

I made a choice. I decided to go with Katherine.

"You had already retained him. How could you switch like that? Didn't you sign an agreement or something?" Woo asked.

I was willing to lose the five hundred dollars versus losing the entire case. I called Jay to inform him of my decision. He was cordial, and he wished me well. I met with Katherine four hours prior to the hearing to retain her. She was nothing like what I had imagined. She was this plain looking, regular and nondescript older White woman. There was nothing outstanding about Katherine. Damn! She's not a Katherine; she's more like a Kate. I like women, but I wouldn't touch that trailer trash looking road whore with a ten foot pole. I thought to myself. We shook each other's hand and sat down to discuss the situation. Her handshake belied her force on the phone as it was weak and placid. Katherine had an aura about her that seemed like a racist cloud to me which was emanated from her. I was not comfortable with her at all, but it was a last minute decision. I had dismissed Jay. I needed an attorney to appear with me so I could get the theft by deception warrant issued.

"Molly, you should have stayed with Jay. What the hell were you thinking, girl!" Woo shouted into the receiver.

"Woo, it's obvious that I wasn't thinking!"

Initially, everything seemed to be going well. One hour after speaking with her and after some deliberation, the true Katherine erupted.

Katherine abruptly stated, "This seems to be a civil issue and not a criminal issue."

"What? Why do you say that?" I asked, and she didn't answer.

During the fact-finding session she spoke with my former

attorney Mike over the phone. She asked him for the email that was sent to him by Rodney, concerning the twenty two hundred dollars. Katherine was completely glossing over the fact that the seven thousand dollars was not theft by deception, but it was a civil offense. Hell, it was quite obvious that Thomas had used the money to cover his outstanding debt to the graphics design company. That was stealing!

"Hell, Yeah. He stole your money!" Woo screamed.

It had gotten down to an hour and a half before court. I was caught in a web of problems. I'm saying to myself, what in the world am I going to do?

Katherine kept saying, "This case is civil and not criminal."

"Why are you just saying this? You didn't say this at the beginning of our conversation?"

She responded, "I kind of felt that way from the beginning."

This was a misrepresentation of the facts. She never told me that she felt that way until an hour into our conversation. She made it appear that it was definitely a criminal case. She even said that she was gonna subpoena Mike to testify. Now it was a different story altogether. It was less than an hour and a half before court. I had told Jay not to appear; now, I was stuck with this country bumpkin hick of an attorney. Hell, Mike literally took my six hundred dollars. I forfeited the five hundred dollars to Jay. There I was sitting in this office with this old witch, who was telling me shit that was completely different from what she said over the phone.

"Can you at least put up a good argument?" I pleaded.

"I don't think the judge will issue a warrant based upon the information that you have," Katherine stated, in her harsh, hoarse, gin and cigarette soaked southern drawl.

Time was not my ally as I had to be in court in one hour. In addition to this dilemma, I had three co-workers meeting me. I needed to meet them to make sure that they arrived in the right courtroom. I just knew that my brother Blake would be there waiting for me. My daddy had spoken to him the week prior.

My daddy said, "I want you to be in that court room with your sister."

Blake responded, "Yes sir. I will."

Well, he wasn't there as promised although I wasn't surprised. I was too mentally tired to try to call Blake and look for my co-workers at the same time. I was having stomach cramps from hell. My head was hurting. It was just so much going on so fast. I knew right then without a shadow of a doubt that I had made a big mistake by replacing Jay with Katherine. I was too involved with her to turn back at such a late stage in the proceedings. At that point, I started preparing myself. It looked as though I was going to be the one convincing the judge of the merits of my case. If I started telling my story from the beginning, omitting the trivial things; mentioning the most important details, it might be just enough to persuade the judge. There was no time to think about the aches and pains. However, while waiting, taking a moment of relaxation before the court proceedings began, I had an epiphany as to how I had arrived there.

{ CHAPTER 8 }

The Set-up by Satan

The previous year, I had begun going to church more. I started attending Bible study classes every Thursday night and church every Saturday. Despite my religion, I sometimes went right back on Sundays. This schedule was the one that I kept for at least three times a month. I even went to the extreme of buying a DVD recorder in order to copy Thursday night's Bible study. I would copy the DVD's and pass them out to strangers who I conversed with. I had a zest to learn the Bible. It was rewarding. My life at the time was equally wonderful.

It was the month of October and Pastor Dale was hosting a special event on the first Thursday night of the month. Hot 105.6, a local urban radio station and a lot of rappers were there. The atmosphere was electric. The event was primarily for teenagers, even though adults attended. Since I went to Bible study on Thursday, this didn't interfere with my schedule. I knew that I had to get there early since this was a big event. I wanted to get a seat in front to be close to the action. When I arrived at church, there was a line of people that stretched around the building. To compound matters, it was about twelve degrees outside. I tried to go into the church using the side door. Since I was a regular patron, I didn't think it would be a problem. I walked up to the side door. A deacon was standing at the door.

"I'm sorry, but you're gonna have to wait in line like everybody else," the deacon said.

"Sir, I can't stand for a long period of time because of my back."

"I'm sorry, but you have to get in line, Miss!"

"Sir, I'm by myself. There's no entourage to worry about."

"Miss, will you step back? I need to shut the door," he said in a rude tone.

"It's freezing cold out here. I see people going in and out!" I said defiantly. "It seems to be ridiculous for me to be standing out here freezing, sir."

The deacon replied, "The ones that are going in and out are doing some type of work."

After standing and waiting for an hour I began to see members of the church bring in friends. I saw faces who were not members. They were coming in and out of the proceedings without being questioned.

"Can I come inside? It seems to be more than just workers being allowed in?"

He said, "No".

I was upset, yet I did speak to him with reason and calmness.

"Sir, I was coming to this church when Pastor Dale was over on the east side speaking from a big podium with a microphone in front of him. There were just a handful of members. I followed him here. I'm known as a regular member. So, you're telling me that I have to stand outside as if I was someone off the streets. I help to build this new church by paying my tithes diligently," I said in a strong and forceful tone.

"I'm sorry, but you still have to get in line, Miss."

After arguing with the Deacon off and on for over two and a half hours, he finally let me in. The church was packed. They were sending people back. By the grace of God, I was able to find a seat in front. Nevertheless, I was so hurt in my spirit by the way I was treated. It bothered me to the point that I couldn't fully enjoy the service. I didn't go back to Bible study nor could I, in good conscience, attend services on Sunday morning. I was so disappointed in the church. I stopped listening to Pastor Dale's sermon tapes. The DVD recorder was a waste of money. After the fiasco with the church, I seemed to drop out of the world of religion completely. I dropped out and then all of my problems seem to drop in. I don't mean that I stopped believing in God. I love Him with all my heart and soul. I simply was slowly, but surely, descending into a pattern of alternately losing, gaining and losing faith in human beings.

After this falling out with the church, I decided to take a trip to New Orleans. While I was there, I consulted with voodoo doctors. There had to be something causing this negative cloud which was hanging over me and causing me so much grief and turmoil. I was sure that someone had done something to me. Maybe someone put a spell on me, an act that old black folks call "putting roots on you". It was hard to justify my belief in God while using an occult practice, but I was desperate. In the war between good and evil that had been waged in my life, evil was winning the battle. I knew at times that I was my own worst enemy; but other times, more than a few, when I had nothing but the best intentions, bad things were still happening.

"I heard those voodoo people were bad, Molly."

"Woo, there're good voodoo doctors and there're bad ones or so I rationalized. I went to the good ones. The 'white magic' purveyors."

"What the hell ever," Woo said while laughing.

I brought this book to read while on the flight called "Voodoo & Hoodoo." It was written by Jim Haskins. In it, he said to be very careful when dealing with different voodoo priests because some male priests will try to take advantage of a female if they know that she is already vulnerable. This happened to me on my visit to New Orleans. A priest tried to bilk me of money as well as my pussy.

I had spoken with one voodoo priest, in particular, numerous times over the phone prior to my decision of taking the trip. I told him that I wanted to take a flight to New Orleans to visit Marie Laveau's grave, since he had mentioned it. According to the priest, Marie Laveau was considered to be the greatest voodoo practitioner in history. There's a belief that her powers even extend beyond the grave. Her followers believe that if you leave three X's on her grave and three pennies, that your request will be granted. Also, if you take a piece of the gravestone, your luck will improve. I had to get there. I was hoping God would forgive me for disobeying Him, this one time. The voodoo priest suggested the trip to the gravesite. He had taken many of his clients to that site, as part of the fee that they paid him. I was gonna proceed with him and my plans hadn't changed until the day before my flight. We had a conversation which revealed his true intentions. I called him less than twenty four hours before my flight.

"I have my flight plans in place. I'm anxious to go to Marie Laveau's grave. Hopefully, this will get this negative curse off of me. When I get to New Orleans, what do I need to do? Do I call you once I get there?" I asked.

"Do you have hotel reservations, yet?" The voodoo priest asked.

I was wondering what in the hell did that matter, but my bullshit detector was beeping inside of my head.

"No, I haven't made any plans like that. I was thinking that I could get a room at a motel or something, that is, if I planned on staying more than a day or so. I was planning on just coming in for the day and leaving. Was there any particular reason why you ask?" I inquired, with my apprehension of his answer making my bullshit meter beep increasingly louder.

"I want you to do me a favor. I want you to get a room at the Marriott," he said, with a voice sounding like a doctor who was giving a patient some medical news which they weren't gonna be pleased with.

"Why do you want me to get a hotel room?' I asked.

"I want to eat your pussy," he said with the same clinical voice as before.

Bingo! The bullshit meter was both flashing and beeping. He was yet another example of how I'd put my trust in another human and the person had an ulterior motive other than helping me.

"You want to eat my pussy? You know I'm gay. What does that have to do with my bad luck? What does eating my pussy have to do with anything?" I asked, being both in shock and anger at the same time.

"Well, I had another client who was gay and after I ate her pussy, she cum so hard she went back to men. She told me that she never cum so hard in her life. So, I think I can cure you from being gay," he said, with the same antiseptic, Cajun-influenced tone which he had maintained during the entire conversation.

"I'll call you when I get to New Orleans, but I have to decline," I said to him as the conversation ended.

I just could not believe that he would be so bold as to think that I was so vulnerable to fall for something like that. I knew I wasn't gonna agree to something that foolish since being gay was not a choice, but it is something that a person is born with and no amount of great oral sex is going to really convert anyone. I love women and that was that. No magical tongue would change that fact. Not even a so-called "syringe tongue."

When I arrived in New Orleans, I managed to find a tour bus that took me to Marie Laveau's gravesite. Now, I could forgo both the fee of the priest and the uncomfortable feeling of being in his presence. I called him just to see if he would answer my call. As I predicted, he did not. The tour bus took me to the gravesite. My plan to draw my X's and leave my three pennies was thwarted by the fact that her grave was completely covered by X's and coins. The trip wasn't completely for nothing; I still made my three wishes. The grave was covered with markings. I managed to mark three X's and left three pennies. There were loose pieces of the grave scattered around. I took a pebble. You could clearly see that there were many people suffering and looking for answers, even from a myth and the remains of a person who was long gone.

"So, you think that your using voodoo may have led to your problems?" Woo asked, with a tone which made the answer seem more rhetorical than anything.

I responded, "I think that first it was because of my frustration over my luck and the second time was because of the case against Thomas. I believed that it opened the door for satan to work his magic and to try to get me to turn even further away from God. I love God and never stopped. I was searching for anything that I thought would work, instead of believing more. I guess that I believed less. My faith was not as strong as I fooled myself to believe that it was. It had gotten weaker. I was trying to rationalize using the occult by claiming that some of it was "white" and some of it was "black." The use of magic and spells is witchcraft regardless of how you try to spin it," I said remorsefully.

"Yep, that's why I don't do that stuff," Woo said in a self-righteous tone.

"Whoa, hold up, you're telling a damn lie! Remember when you had that Oija board? You were talking to some spirit. You even let me ask a question and that fucking pointer thing moved over to answer the question. I asked the spirit who he was. He told me David by spelling it out. It's a good thing that I had an evangelist to come over and bless them demons out of my place!" I barked in a semi-serious yet playful tone.

"You're fucking kidding me, Molly. You had someone to go over there and do an exorcism on your condo! That's wild as hell." Woo laughed hysterically.

"Hey, that shit is serious. I'll get to that in time. One thing I've learned is that you can't serve two masters. I was doing that by calling myself a God fearing person and at the same time using the satanic principles of magic and witchcraft. I learned a lot from that. Let me get back to this story," I said.

Finally, I could see clearly as I mentally prepared for my ordeal in court. I clearly was a victim/ product/ purveyor of seduction on many levels. Using money, power, or words, these shysters twisted to coin a phrase. It was as if my life was flashing back in Cliff notes. I went back thirty years to my affiliations with Willie Mae and Nicole, and my seduction of Sonya Stanfordson and similar events. Then I move forward in time to Thomas. I saw how satan had used my tendencies to be a willing participant in my own woes as a weapon against me. I had probably seen signs in that church which suggested that they would treat me the way they did. I ignored the signs and became ultimately disillusioned. I can't say that I was unaware of what was occurring in my life. In practically every case, I allowed myself to become a party to the events which have shaped my life, even though my better judgment was telling me to do otherwise. However, through my sheer gullibility and naiveté, I was at once the cause of and a victim of my circumstances.

"Nawh, I think those fuckers are all crooks. You're just another one of their victims," Woo said.

"Let me get back to the court scene," I said.

I met my co-workers a short distance from the courthouse. I was very weak in both spirit and flesh. I couldn't keep saying that to myself because I didn't want to make the situation worse. We had a quick lunch. I had to leave. I tried to give them accurate directions. I didn't want them to be even a minute late. Once I arrived at the courtroom I waited outside. I wasn't feeling comfortable with Katherine. I had a thousand thoughts circling throughout my mind at one time. I began to feel panicky. So, I attempted to dial Attorney Jay's number. As soon as I dialed the damn number, Katherine walked up to me. I turned the phone off immediately. I knew that Jay's office was only ten minutes away. So, I was gonna try to make a last ditch attempt to secure him. Once again, I had gone against my instincts. I had to suffer for it. It was five minutes before court started. I was sitting on the front bench with Katherine. My co-workers were sitting behind us. The courtroom was beginning to fill up. I kept looking around for Thomas and his attorney, but I didn't see them. This was a good sign. He only had five more minutes to get there. If he didn't show up the judge would issue the warrant.

The judge came into the courtroom. The roll call began. Thomas was not in attendance. I was so damn happy. My name was called. Katherine answered for me. To my surprise, Thomas's attorney stood up and answered for him. I thought, Damn! Ok, he's still not here. So, that's still good. I was so nervous. The roll call was completed. The judge called our case first. I went up before the judge alone with Katherine. Thomas's attorney also approached the bench.

Katherine said, "Your Honor, we are having subpoena problems."

Thomas's attorney replied, "Your Honor, my client is not here yet."

The judge said, "I'll give you a little time to step outside and try to resolve this."

At that point I said to myself, why didn't Katherine ask for the warrant? I sat back down. Both attorneys went outside. After waiting for fifteen minutes, I went outside to see what the problem was. Thomas's attorney was on the phone, more than likely trying to reach him. Katherine was standing in the general area not far away from Thomas's green-eyed lawyer. He reminded me so much of my neighbor's little green-eyed bad ass boy from West Palm. I stared at him for a minute.

I wondered if he was Jeremy, I thought. If he is Jeremy all grown up, I am in trouble.

I asked Katherine, "Why don't you ask for a bench warrant?"

She responded, "The judge is not going to issue a warrant."

"Katherine, how can you be so sure of what the judge will decide?"

She said, "I know."

After forty-five minutes, Thomas still hadn't arrived at court. My co-worker, Mrs. Hall, decided to leave. She said that the process was taking too long. Bonnie, my other co-worker that was in attendance, wanted to leave with her, but I managed to persuade her to stay. Finally, Thomas's big ass came strolling and rolling in. He was fifty minutes late.

"It would seem to me that a bench warrant should have been automatically given," Woo said.

"Well, it wasn't."

"Your attorney should have asked for one to be issued right away with her stupid ass," Woo said angrily.

Incredibly, Thomas's attorney, Jeremy Wellman, came over to Katherine with a settlement. He offered two thousand dollars and all the rights to my modeling agency.

I said, "NO!"

Jeremy was a young dude. He was probably in his early thirties. We then went back in to court. Most of the cases were over. The courtroom was half empty.

"I don't blame you. I would have said no, too. How in the hell can someone take seven thousand dollars and turn right around and say, I'll give you two thousand of your own money back? That's pure bullshit!" Woo shouted.

"Woo, it was ALL bullshit."

The judge asked us to approach the bench.

The judge said, "I looked over these papers. I'm trying to figure out how is this a criminal case?"

I responded quickly, "You Honor, can I give you the circumstances surrounding the case?"

I began to speak. Katherine whispered to me, "Stick to the facts."

After this action of arm grabbing and ear whispering, I couldn't finish what I had to say. I felt that the judge needed to hear the beginning of what happened in order to fully understand. I knew when Thomas took the stand he was going to be quite convincing. Katherine asked me two inconsequential questions. She entered a piece of paper as exhibit one. Mr. Wellman then asked me several questions. In contrast to him, Katherine was clearly overmatched. One of the questions was concerning the graphic designer, Rodney. He was subpoenaed, but failed to appear. I tried to speak to the facts of exhibit one which was the email sent to me. Thomas had stated in the email that he was going to pay me out of his personal account. Wellman objected, calling it no more than "hearsay." The judge agreed and sustained his motion. My testimony lasted no longer than five minutes.

Now, it was Thomas's turn to testify. Thomas went up to the bench struggling because of his weight. More than likely he was probably out of breath because he was running late. The judge asked him about exhibit one. Thomas told the judge that when he wrote the email he was under duress. The judge asked him what kind of duress was he was alluding to. Thomas began to speak with his so soft voice and soothing tone. He should have been an actor. This man was so dramatic!

Thomas said, "Your Honor, Molly was calling me early in the morning. She wanted to bring nude pictures of herself over for me to see them. You see, she was trying to date me. Molly also has under age females living with her. She prostitutes them out to older men. One was killed. She also has businessmen coming over for the girls. She's like a madam or a pimp, selling the girls for sex. Molly called me last Friday, You Honor. She said that she was coming over to the office. I told her that it was Phyllis's birthday and I was thinking of her, even though she's no longer here."

"Who is Phyllis?" The judge asked.

"She was my wife, Your Honor. She passed away earlier this year."

At that point he started to cry crocodile tear, like a little bitch! The tears were just streaming down his face. I was mad as a dog with rabies!

Thomas said, "I kept telling Molly it was Phyllis's birthday. Can't I just grieve? You Honor, Molly said that she grieves every day because she had recently lost her mother. Your Honor, Molly also wanted to include sex acts with animals for the photo shoots with the models," he said crying.

"That Big Lying Assed Bastard of a Bitch!" Woo shouted.

I was standing there looking at him in complete amazement. The people in the courtroom were also staring at him as if to say "that big fucker is crazy as hell." There's no way anyone can say anything like that and still be considered sane. I was so upset upon hearing Thomas tell those horrendous lies. My co-workers, who were there to testify on my behalf, said that I turned bloody red. It takes a truly sick mind to think of sex acts with animals, as well as to accuse someone of such things. I could never say that, think that, nor could I accuse my worst enemy of something so putrid. That was indicative of the extremes to which Thomas would go to gain his own end. This was the sickest shit I've ever heard of in my life! It literally made me sick to my stomach, to hear him lie like that AND to include bestiality!

The judge said, "That's enough, I don't want to hear anymore."

I started to speak quickly, but I was cut off at "Your Honor." I was grabbed by the arm again by Katherine, who whispered in my ear, That's ok.

The judge said to me, "I'm not saying that you are not going to get your money back, but I'm sending this over to civil court."

Are you punishing me for the things that I had done in my past? I asked God.

"That bastard told all of those nasty lies on you and your lawyer didn't object even once?" Woo asked, with a fervor of curiosity.

"Naw, ol' trailer park Kate didn't say a damn word," I sighed.

That big bitch could have won an Oscar for his performance as a frightened victim. The lies rolled off his tongue like nectar. It was one lie after another and each one was so seamless, that to the casual observer they would have seemed plausible. In all my years on this earth, I had never seen anyone lie so well. I knew right then, and beyond a shadow of a doubt, that Thomas killed Phyllis. I was ninety five percent sure before this fiasco in court, but now I was one hundred percent sure.

I only imagined the torment poor Phyllis was put through. As far as the family goes, I know they went through pure hell dealing with Thomas. No wonder they were hesitant about following through with the investigation. They knew what kind of hellion that they would be facing. They would have been facing satan himself. This man was totally consumed with and possessed by evil. I had met Beelzebub way back in 2003 and didn't know it. Thomas was nothing but pure evil, nothing but deceit and lies and full of hurt. The only conclusion was maybe something happened back in his childhood that we may never know. Perhaps, he was possessed and the demon continues to rule him. There's no way a person could speak of all of these things and not have done or considered them, at some point in their past. Thomas most certainly had done many evil things and had gotten away with them. He was much too clever and too good at what he did, to have not made a practice of deceiving and manipulation. Maybe his family was grifters, gypsies, con artists and maybe this is how he learned.

"Woo, Maggie did say that Thomas's mother wanted him to get rid of Phyllis because she was too sickly," I said.

"It definitely makes you wonder. What happened to his real father, hunh?"

"What do you mean by that?" I asked.

Woo laughed and said, "You do remember the movie FRIED GREEN TOMATOS?"

"Aw'ight, I get it! Hot water and a big stirring stick," we both started laughing out loud.

"I'm glad you finally got to the murder part, Damn!"

"Ok Missy, calm down there's more."

Later that night after court, I was visiting one of my co-workers, Mark, at his home. I received two phone calls on my cell phone. We were watching television at the time and not really doing much else, other than making small talk about work and keeping each other company. It was from Thomas. I couldn't believe that this fat bastard was still calling me. During the second call, he actually threatened to kill me and my dog.

He said, "There's no way I'm gonna let you destroy what I worked so hard for."

"Unt unh, no Donkey Kong didn't call you after all that bull shit in court. So, what the hell he work so hard for?" Woo asked.

"What do you think Woo?"

"Work hard to steal and kill," Woo replied.

"Yeah, Aw'ight then," I finally said.

We had the television up so loud on the first call that all I could hear was a male voice cursing. So, I hung up. He called back a second time. So, I turned the speakerphone on so that Mark could hear.

"Mark said, "Call 911."

A police officer came out to Mark's home and took a report. We then took the report over to the judge on duty. I asked for an application hearing on phone threats. The judge looked at the report and gave me a court date for the next week. That same day, I called Jay, and told him about what had happened. He told me that I should go and retrieve the application for phone threats, because it would look like an act of retaliation toward Thomas. I immediately called the clerk's office and luckily the document had not gone out in the mail. I called Mark, my co-worker, and I asked him to meet me at the courthouse. Attorney Jay advised me to apply for a restraining order against Thomas. Mark met me at the courthouse. While we were in the hallway filling out the paper work for the restraining order, before we went before the judge, a sharp looking Hispanic man walked up with a brief case in his hands.

"Excuse me. Can I have one of your cards?" I asked.

"Sure."

"How do you pronounce your name?"

"Del Joseph."

"What would you charge to represent me in a civil case filed in state court?"

"What is the case about?"

"It's a difficult case dealing with a conniving con artist."

Then, I went into small bits of details.

He said, "I'll charge you eleven hundred dollars."

I was shocked by his price because Jay had quoted me a price of five thousand to take my case to state court.

I asked, "Does the price include the whole process of going before the jury?"

"Yes."

I asked, "How much will you charge me to get this restraining order taken care of?"

He said, "Two hundred fifty dollars."

"I only have one hundred-fifty dollars."

"That's fine," he said.

"Can you get the edict extended for more than ten days?"

He responded, "That won't be a problem."

The court attendant called us in and the judge asked questions. I told him about the application for a warrant that was held on the day prior. The judge then set the hearing date for the following week.

I kept slightly bumping Del Joseph with my arm; Katherine style.

Del Joseph finally asked, "Your Honor, can we extend the date?"

The judge said, "No, we have to hear these cases in ten days."

Hell, I could have saved that hundred and fifty dollars. I can see in looking back on that decision to hire Del Joseph, that once again, I was swayed by my assumptions based on the superficial. I had seen a well dressed man who looked the part and I went with style over substance. This tendency has not served me well with many of my decisions throughout my life. Del Joseph set up the appointment for me to come by his office. Thomas's calling me while I was visiting Mark apparently wasn't enough as he called me back two days later. I was at my doctor's office at the time. I purposefully had the speaker phone on, so the nurse could be a witness.

He said, "Britney is going to meet you, to give you the money."

I yelled, "Thomas don't you ever call me again!"

I hung up and dialed 911. The police came and took a report. The nurse who overheard Thomas could not come to the hearing for the restraining order. She had to work for someone else who was out on sick leave. I was out of luck once more, since Thomas had made the one call that I could have used to secure a harassment conviction on him. It seemed to me as though Thomas had some kind of supernatural force protecting him. I needed answers to whatever it was, that was helping him.

I headed back to New Orleans once again on the following day, to seek out some supernatural help of my own. I took another trip to voodoo priestess Marie Laveau's grave to make a wish for protection. In my mind, I could see no other way but to fight fire with occult flames. I kept the report of the call that Thomas made, so I could give it to Del Joseph on the following week before the court appearance. I tried calling Del Joseph to let him know about the phone call, but he didn't answer my call. I thought nothing of it when he didn't answer, at that time.

"Molly, the voodoo didn't work the first time, so why you went back?"

"Shit, I don't know."

That night before the trip, I had some strange things to occur, such as a flickering of my computer monitor even though the power was off. The vision of a tall and dark apparition had come to see me three or four times. I could only conclude that Phyllis was trying to tell me something, if she was in fact the spirit who was making herself visible to me. I'm sure that it was, because it all started when the conflict with Thomas began. Needless to say, I had very little sleep that night. Maybe Phyllis was trying to keep me from making the trip.

Years ago, I would hear old people say things that you should and shouldn't do, as far as superstitions of good or bad luck was concerned. They would talk about cooking certain foods on New Year's Day for good luck, breaking mirrors or what certain weather signs meant among other signs. Most of these things were included in Jim Haskin's "Voodoo and Hoodoo" book, which I again had with me during that flight to New Orleans. I had only read a small portion of the book on my previous trip to visit Marie Laveau's grave, so I finished it on the second flight.

As I had alluded to before, as a child and even until this very day, I can see visions of the departed. Sometimes when I see an apparition, something would happen afterwards, as if the spirit was warning me about something. I was always too afraid to try and communicate with the spirit. I was literally scared out of my panties when they would appear. I was hoping that the spirit of Phyllis or whoever it was, was not warning me of something.

I knew that the visions were happening, but I wasn't sure about what was really going on because I honestly did not understand WHY they were happening. Why was I burdened with this ability/curse of seeing spirits and the inconvenience of never sleeping with the lights off? I saw my Grandma Lenora's spirit two months after her burial as clearly as if she was standing in front of me alive. I'll never forget that night when it happened. I was lying in the bed unable to sleep, I opened my eyes and grandma was sitting on my mother's bed looking right at me.

"Mama, Mama, Mama," I screamed.

"Baby, what's wrong?" Mama asked.

"I saw grandma!"

"Baby, grandma is dead. You were just having a bad dream," Mama said. "You go back to sleep."

"No, mama. I saw grandma. She was sitting right there looking at me!"

"Grandma is dead, baby."

"Mama, she had these little curls all over her head and she had this white dress on and it had a fluffy collar!"

Mama's eyes grew real big, because she knew that there was no way I could have known this. Mama never doubted me from that day forward. My mother had the funeral home to curl my grandmother's hair into little Shirley Temple curls. Grandma's hair was never in curls before her death. When I told my mother about the little curls in grandma's hair, she knew that this was the only way I could have known.

"Baby, don't you be afraid. Maybe she was trying to tell you something."

"Mama, I don't want to hear what she has to say! I'm scared!"

I was always terrified of them, whether they were trying to tell me something that I needed to know or not. Long ago my mother revealed to me the nature of my power/curse.

"Baby, you were born with a veil over your face."

I asked her, "Mama, what is a veil?"

She said, "It's a very thin, wet, transparent layer of membrane covering the face. The doctor had to peel it off, but it came off easily."

I never really understood what that meant as a child, however she told me that story more than three or four times. I can only guess that she didn't want me to ever forget that point.

I didn't. I remembered telling this to a very spiritual lady at work by the name of Mrs. Tex, who was an evangelist in her other vocation outside of the postal service.

"Mrs. Tex, my mama told me that I was born with a veil over my face."

After I told her about my auspicious birth, she looked at me with her wide eyes and said, "Why would your mother tell you that? It's a curse to be able to see the departed!"

I let that statement go into one ear and out of the other. I knew that my mother was a very spiritual lady and her mere words did not bring the ability to me, but rather an act of God did. When I had problems, I would ask my mother her opinion, she would always say "Baby, don't worry about it, the Lord will take care of it." It was always the Lord. If anyone in my life was speaking words with the power of God, it was my mother.

During this second flight to New Orleans, I had now read the entire Haskin's book more extensively. Even Haskins reiterated in his writings that long-standing supernatural belief of the veil. He wrote in his book that when a person was born with a veil over her face, then that person is a special person on a psychic level. Those who were veiled were able to summon spirits and communicate with them. Unfortunately, wayward spirits gravitate toward them. My eyes got very big and my heart began to beat rapidly. "Wow! Mama was right! I am a blessing!" Now, it was clear to me why Phyllis was coming to me. She was trying to use me in order to tell her story, so that Thomas would be prosecuted and that justice would be served.

Once again I visited Marie Laveau's grave and asked her departed spirit for help. I again made my three wishes and knocked on her grave three times and left three pennies, just as the ritual prescribed. I brought another piece of cement from her grave. It's amazing that her grave is still standing. You can tell that many pieces had been taken. You would think that voodoo is predominantly a black person's belief, but that is far from the truth. In fact, I could barely get into these places, because there were so many white people in front of me. There were so many whites in that graveyard. I couldn't believe what I was seeing. The Haskins book stated that white and other ethnicities feel comfortable visiting sites such as this, when they're in New Orleans.

"Molly, you know, nothing unites the races more than common suffering."

"Yeah, you right. 9-11 and Katrina were the scariest days for me."

"For me, too," Woo said sadly.

"Wasn't you in jail on that day?"

"Just get back to the story. P-l-e-a-s-e!" Woo said with agitation.

I had believed with all of my heart, the weekend trip was going to be successful and that a deceased voodoo priestess would grant my wishes and vanquish the evil which had tormented me for years. I was hoping that the good of the "white voodoo" was acceptable. I was not seeking to place a spell on or wish ill on anyone, not even Thomas. I simply wanted some forces of the universe, whether it be good or bad, to exact justice upon him.

I returned home late that evening, so I could be well rested for the next day. It was the day of court. I was about to put the effectiveness of my wish to Marie Laveau's grave to the test, once again. One of my wishes was that the wrongs and injustices of my life be made right or avenged. It was a known fact that this particular county judge didn't stand for foolishness and histrionics. So, Thomas wasn't about to get in front of this judge and give another acting performance. I felt pretty good about going back to court. I arrived on time. I had my representation, Del Joseph. Thomas had a different attorney this time, not ol' green-eyes.

He involved poor Britney and Tracey into this mess once again. It was obvious, that this man had brain washed these young girls. Where were their families in the midst of all of this? Did the families of the young girls even know that he told them to lie under oath? Britney didn't know about the lack of respect that Thomas had for her. He was literally using her as a lackey. I remembered asking Thomas what would happen to the business, if something should ever happen to him.

"Tracey will take over the business," Thomas replied.

"Why wouldn't Britney be your first choice?"

He replied, "I liked Tracey better than Britney."

Not only was Thomas a liar and a con man, he had absolutely no loyalty. He was a perfect example of that old adage — there is no honor among thieves. Court began. We had a male judge. The first thing Thomas's attorney did was to hand the Judge a piece of paper.

"This will help you with the pronunciation of my last name, because everybody has problems saying it," he said.

In reality, he was trying to name drop with the judge in order to influence him. The piece of paper had the law firm's letterhead on it. He was an Italian and the judge appeared to be also, which may have played into his judgment as anyone might infer. He was smart to recognize that the judge probably didn't recognize his name from any random lawyer. The law firm was a major firm based in that county. He probably scored style points. My attorney didn't catch on to his astute tactical thinking at all.

My case was on the docket first. I took the stand. My attorney began to ask me questions. I answered to the best of my ability. However, his questions to me were strangely vague. I did get the opportunity to go into detail briefly about the entire ordeal before Thomas's attorney objected. Thomas's attorney cross-examined me. His attorney seemed to ask relevant and compelling questions. Del Joseph didn't tell me to bring a copy of my phone records, to show that Thomas had called and threatened me. As my counsel, he should have made sure that I was prepared.

The judge said, "I'm not going to issue a restraining order, because I'm not going to count the first phone call. She admitted that she really couldn't hear the call clearly. In order for it to be deemed as harassment, the filer must have received more than one call."

Damn! I needed that nurse here with me to testify!

Thomas's attorney said, "Your honor, we are requesting attorney fees."

The judge said, "No, because I'm not totally convinced that the calls weren't made."

I was glad of that decision, but the judge also said "I don't want to see either of you in my court room again." As we were leaving out of the courtroom, Thomas once again put on his victim's act, by making pitiful faces and crying. I overheard him say aloud, "She keeps bothering me, what can I do to stop her?" The same crocodile tears were streaming down his fat cheeks, but this time no one was listening. Suddenly, the judge looked at Thomas and said, "Mr., you were lucky this time." What exactly was the judge trying to say? It appeared as though he could see the guilt clearly, but he was cutting Thomas a break.

"If that was the case then his decision was a complete crock of shit," Woo implied.

"They all were full of shit!"

"Molly, is the court system listed on the stock exchange?"

"Is your real-estate company listed? Why you ask me that stupid ass question? If you're tired, just say so."

"I was just kidding you, child."

"Woo, how you gonna be kidding me when I'm telling you something that's serious? By the way, I'm glad that you finally stopped shaking your ass."

"P-l-e-a-s-e, go on with the story."

The voodoo priest told me to wear black and red to court and to leave candles burning at strategic points in my home. Even though I followed all of the voodoo protocol, it had absolutely no effect, whatsoever. If someone had to be declared a winner in the proceedings, it would have been Thomas. He escaped his terrorist threats and he still had my damned money. After the court proceedings, we stood outside for at least twenty minutes talking about the judge and what had been said. Thomas and his crew were in the back of the hallway for about twenty minutes. I couldn't hear what they were saying, but his facial gestures and the fake sobbing suggested that he was telling another of his endless lies.

"Is that your phone beeping, Woo?"

"Yes, but I'm not gonna answer. Just go on with the story."

I went to Del Joseph's office the following day to retain him and file the seemingly never ending lawsuit against Thomas. I mentioned that Mike had taken six hundred dollars from me and didn't show up for court. He told me to write Mike a letter and if he didn't respond to contact the bar association. This was the first time the bar association crossed my mind. I retained Del Joseph for a fee of eleven hundred dollars. The check was cashed the next day. He told me that he was going to type up the lawsuit against Thomas. He said that he would call me in a week, so that I could look it over and sign it. After a week went by, I called him. He didn't return my calls.

In the mean time, Thomas's attorney sent me a small amount of the so-called "work" that Thomas had done for so many hours. He wanted me to believe that all of my money had been spent on a pamphlet. I was so pissed off. I once again went to work doing my own investigating. This time, I uncovered new evidence over the internet against Thomas from a model named Marie. She was one of the models Thomas used in the four page pamphlet which he called a "proposal package". Through correspondences, I persuaded Marie to send me all the e-mails she had received from Thomas. Marie said that she had tried to contact Thomas after she sent pictures to him, but she couldn't reach him.

I then called The Express Ink Company in Valletta, which is the company he used to print the information. I discovered that, despite spending my seven thousand dollars and supposedly spending countless hours to make up the so-called "proposal package." It only cost Thomas a whopping twenty eight dollars, to make the four page pamphlet. I also found out that he picked up the four page calendar/pamphlet on the day he was fifty minutes late for court. He was late because Express Ink didn't have the calendar completed. He had done no work prior to this day, but he wasn't taking any chances on not having it just in case the judge asked him to see the work that he called himself completing.

All of the models he allegedly contracted to appear on the proposal package for the investors, were models that he had gotten off of the website "MySpace". The damning evidence was that he perpetrated an illegal act by using the women's pictures without their permission. I even contacted one of the "models" who turned out to be a plastic surgeon. Her name was Vanessa Grooves. She informed me that she had never spoken to Thomas and was extremely surprised to see her face plastered on the pamphlet. To make matters even more damning, he also took the names of their photographers off of their photographs, to make it appear as though the "modeling agency" had photographed the models. He copied editorial work from published articles. Everything was word for word plagiarism. He made it appear as though he had researched the information.

He committed plagiarism, copyright infringement, and fraud to the ninth degree. I could not fathom how a man who committed such blatant illegal acts was never caught or punished. He had lied to get a higher level job, murdered his wife by overdosing her with painkillers, swindled me out of thousands of dollars, committed slander on record at the court by accusing me of bestiality, and now, he had stolen material from the internet and was attempting to profit from it. All the while, he acted as though he was some persecuted victim. It was just incredible!

"Got Damn, Molly!" Woo said in a loud tone.

I made an appointment with Attorney Cathy. Cathy was the attorney I had spoken with during the time I was scurrying back and forth to find last minute representation. I met with Cathy on a Saturday at her home in Valletta. I was trying to get her to reapply for the application warrant for theft by deception against Thomas, based on the new evidence. We sat down. I told her everything that was going on with the case. She said to me words that should have shocked me, yet at that point I was jaded to almost everything.

She said, "I'm not going to take your money, Molly. I run

my business out of my home as you can see. I represent drug dealers and other criminal types. So morally, I can't afford to take someone's money and not represent them properly."

Once again, the sound or appearance of a person had caused me to form an opinion before actually knowing them. As was with other lawyers who I had encountered, she sounded the part. I made the same mistake with Katherine, assuming that the aggressive nature of her voice meant that she would represent me better than Jay. I solicited the counsel of Del Joseph because he was dressed in a nice suit and he looked the part of a competent lawyer.

I learned a valuable lesson throughout all of this, that was, not to make snap decisions. I had to allow myself the opportunity to find out who I was putting my trust in. This was something that I had failed to do on so many other occasions in my life. It had cost me. Fortunately, Cathy was an exception to that rule.

Cathy said, "Call Del Joseph on Monday. If he doesn't answer his phone, leave a message saying that you will be by his office to get your eleven hundred dollars back." Then she said, "Tell him, if he doesn't give it back that you'll be contacting the bar association to report him."

This was the second time, I had heard about the bar association. I did exactly what she said.

That Monday morning came. I called Del Joseph and he didn't answer his phone. I got dressed and went by his office. I parked my car and walked toward his building. Before I got to the steps, he came out of his building with his briefcase in hand. Del Joseph saw me standing there motionless waiting on him. I stared at him. I knew he could see anger in my eyes. I was mad as hell.

"I filed your lawsuit on Friday, I have not returned your

calls because I was out of town," he said making forced eye contact with me.

"I just left the courts and they told me that the lawsuit was not filed. So, how could you have filed it, if you were out of town?" I asked.

"I got someone else to do it for me," he said.

"Well, that someone else should have told you that he didn't file it, because it's not filed," I said while my eyes were burning through him as though I was an X-ray machine.

"Okay. Then, I will go to the court to file it now."

"Mr. Joseph, I'm not going through this with another attorney. I need for you to give me something in writing right now, saying that you will represent this case through the entire process in state court for the fee we agreed on of eleven hundred dollars," I said firmly.

Del Joseph didn't hesitate. He wrote all the information that I requested on a receipt and handed it to me. I didn't care what he wrote it on as long as he knew that I wasn't playing. I just felt like fighting that morning when I saw him. At that point, I was tired of the shabby treatment that I had received from these lawyers. I had paid them my money to represent me and they acted as if they were doing it pro bono. Del Joseph knew I was calling his ass repeatedly and he purposefully didn't call me back. He was acting like a real arrogant son-of-a-bitch.

Del Joseph finally filed the paperwork.

He sent me an email that stated that he had filed the papers. "The young lady who filed the papers was new and accidentally filed them in superior court instead of state," he said. I emailed him back and said, God knew which court he wanted it in. Maybe he was not religious, but I wanted to let him know that I was putting my faith in God, despite my paradoxically using voodoo, to try and solve my legal woes. In the meantime, I filed a grievance with the bar association on attorney Mike, for taking my six hundred dollars as a retainer and not showing up for court. Also, I filed on Katherine for not properly representing me. I got a response back from the state bar.

"You didn't waste anytime and I'm glad that you didn't!" Woo said.

"I don't have a problem filing a grievance against an attorney who doesn't properly represent me and who will intentionally take my money!" I said.

"Yeah, more people need to stop walking away from cases after poor representation, and bitching 'bout how sorry their attorney was without taking action," Woo responded.

I stated, "To me, if someone feels that she was shortchanged, then she should file a grievance against those unscrupulous shysters. If not, the hucksters will keep doing the same screw job to other unsuspecting rubes."

"Yep, this is exactly the reason why innocent people are sitting in prison to this day. It's because of improper representation."

"Woo, the bottom line is, some lawyers just don't give a shit about you."

"Some don't give a shit 'bout nothing!" Woo said out loud.

I received two letters from the bar association denying both grievances. I wasn't at all surprised at the bar's decision, since they're a fraternity of men and women of the same profession.

"Hell Naw! They denied your grievance?" Woo yelled.

"Yup."

That's when I decided to go back to the internet to find out what other things this monster, Thomas, had perpetrated. This time, I visited county courts. I managed to find all the civil cases in Georgia that involved Thomas. One case involved Thomas Walters vs. Phyllis Walters. Thomas had taken out a protective order with the court against Phyllis. It was granted for seven months. There were three witnesses to support him in the filing. The persons were Thomas's mother, a woman named Donna and Maggie. So, I decided to call Maggie.

I asked, "Maggie, did you ever write a letter for Thomas to help him get a protective order against Phyllis?"

"I never wrote a letter for Thomas. Maybe he put something in front of me, without telling me the full nature of it and I signed it without knowing what it was," she said with the usual naïve tone to her voice.

"Maggie, would you really sign something without reading it first?" I asked.

"Molly, I'm in my car on the way home," she said. "I'll call you as soon as I get home."

Maggie didn't call me back that afternoon, so I decided to call her back. I managed to reach her. I gave her the site information before she could say that she would call me back again. To be honest, she seemed reluctant and even somewhat combative about taking it.

"I'm not going to look at it today," Maggie said. "I have to answer my EEOC case, but I will look at it tomorrow and give you a call."

The next day came and I never received a call from Maggie. So that's when I decided to speak with my co-workers, Bonnie and Mrs. Hall, about Maggie. They were aware of the situation. We all agreed that this did not sound plausible. We were also in agreement on the fact that Maggie should have been more curious about something she wasn't aware of agreeing to. Three days later, Maggie finally called me. She started talking about her father's illness. I switched the conversation, not because I didn't want to hear about her father, but because I wanted to get to the truth. I asked if she had visited the site. She said no.

I said, "Maggie, if you want me to, I'll go and make a copy of the letter."

She responded, "No, I don't want you to go out of your way. I'll get it."

I didn't say anything. At that point, I knew that she was lying. I then decided that I needed to go and get a copy of the letter, before it mysteriously went missing from the file. In the mean time, I receive an email from Del Joseph and it read, Thomas agreed to pay you five thousand dollars and give you the rights to Ten Cents Modeling Agency. I didn't respond right away. After having a wonderful weekend, I had a moment of reality and clarity. I began to question myself as well as the situation in general. I asked myself, Why should I believe Thomas is gonna pay me any of my money? Hell, he had gone back on his word before? At that point, I called Del Joseph. Once again, he didn't answer the phone. I sent him an email. In the correspondence, I asked him when would I get my money. That same day, he returned my call.

"Hello, Molly. How are you?"

"Del Joseph, why is it taking so long for me to get my money?"

"I gave Attorney Wellman a week's extension," Del Joseph said.

"For what?"

"The reason I granted the extension was because Wellman is going to type up the agreement," Del Joseph responded.

"It doesn't take a week to write up an agreement?" I said, in a tone which suggested that I was fed up with both him and all of the bullshit surrounding him.

"He asked for a week, so I didn't see a problem," he muttered.

"Don't you remember that Thomas had agreed to pay me before and he didn't?" I asked.

"I know that, but his attorney said that both he and Thomas are ready to get this thing over with."

"Ok, Mr. Joseph, I'm telling you that Thomas is a tremendous liar and he's gonna try to get out of this."

We hung up. I decided to call down to the superior court. I found out that the extension was granted for two weeks instead of one week. I immediately sent Del Joseph an email asking him why he said that the extension was for one week. I got neither returned calls from him nor returned emails. I kept calling his ass over and over until my fingers were nearly numb. Finally, I got a copy of an email from Del Joseph, with an attachment from Wellman, which in turn attached an email from Thomas, to me. Thomas had the audacity to request "in addition to the agreement, I want a formal apology from Molly because she said that I called her and threatened to kill her and her dog.

I was mad as hell!

I sent Del Joseph an email stating, "Don't ever send me a third or fourth party email from this man! You know what he put me through, and yet you forward emails to me from him? You shoulda known that this was a stall tactic from the damn beginning."

He did not respond.

It woulda been the ultimate insult for me to apologize for something he did, to ME. If I had apologized to him just to get my money and to put an end to the case, Thomas could have called me a week later, threatened me again, and I couldn't expect anyone to believe me. Through an apology, I would basically have said that I harassed him. Anything I said afterwards about him harassing me would have zero credibility. Really, if you think about it, Thomas could have done anything that he wanted to me at that point and gotten away with it. I would probably have ended up somewhere behind bars fooling around with Thomas's fat lying ass. Thomas knew exactly what he was doing and I wasn't falling for it.

"Molly, that was just a scheme until he got his way. Your lawyer shoulda been a little sharper than that!" Woo said, raising her voice somewhat for emphasis.

"My lawyer didn't give a shit about me, Woo!"

A couple of days later, I received a letter in the mail from Thomas's attorney. It was just what I thought, another stunt to blur the truth once again. It was an answer filed to my lawsuit, instead of an agreement to settle the case. On that same day, I had called down to the clerks of the courts. I called all day up until the court closed. They said that they had not received a response from Wellman. I asked all three clerks of all three courts, if they had gotten anything concerning my case, they kept saying NO!

Magically at 4:00 pm, the answer showed up. I questioned it, but they all said that it could have been pushed deeply down into a basket of files. That was bullshit. They back dated the answer to the lawsuit, but I couldn't prove it. Del Joseph never intended to take my case through the entire procedure. He was just looking for a way out. I then emailed him yet again, after calling and going by his office several times. Finally, I wrote an email saying, I will be at the bar on Monday morning to file a complaint.

That was what Del Joseph was waiting to hear. That was his way out. He didn't waste any time filing a withdrawal from my case. My speculation was that he had done many clients this way. He knew that a lawyer could take his client's money and withdraw from the case, at any point in time. A lawyer who sincerely cares for his clients wouldn't ever dream of this, but assholes like him would.

"Girl, they all saw you coming!" Woo said.

They all heard my story. In the back of their minds, instead of listening to me, they were thinking, How can I take advantage of her too?

Now, as I look back, I remembered sitting in Del Joseph's office. When I asked him a question, all his responses were either yes or no. He never spoke. I did all of the talking. All the while, he knew that he wasn't gonna take my case all the way through to a jury trial for eleven hundred dollars.

Woo stated, "I truly believe Thomas offered Wellman a piece of profit share and he felt obligated past the point of his being a client."

"He offered profit share to every damn body, didn't he?" I responded.

"Yeah, he did, but I imagined Maggie didn't get hers like he promised, obviously." We chuckled.

I received a certified letter from Del Joseph along with all my documents saying he was withdrawing from my case. I knew it was coming. He formally made a request to the judge. I had ten days to file a response. I sat down and wrote out the response along with my concerns, asking the judge to deny his request. The next day, I took it down to the superior court to file it. I didn't have any idea of what I was doing, but it didn't stop me. I asked the clerk for help. The clerk told me right away that they couldn't give out any legal advice. I stood there wondering, if I was filing the correct information. I met with another attorney named Horace. I asked him to take over my case. He advised me that he couldn't discuss my case, since Del Joseph was still my attorney on file. Hell, I waited an entire week to hear him say that shit. What he stated to me was a pure unadulterated lie, because I found out later, through the judge's law clerk, that an attorney can submit a 'substitute for an attorney' application.

"He didn't have to lie," Woo stated. "He shoulda said he wasn't interested in taking your case."

"Am I just a magnet for these people? Are most lawyers this way? Is Karma for my past transgressions coming home to roost?" I asked. "At any rate, the wishes that I made at Marie Laveau's grave didn't change my situation one iota," I said.

"Wow, man, you had some terrible luck with those people!" Woo quipped. "You really wasted that money that you spent on that voodoo trip, didn't cha?"

"Pretty much. I probably woulda been better served by just putting that money into a church. I woulda had the same results if I had just handed it to a bum on the street," I said trying to make a joke of the situation, but in reality I knew what I had said was true.

"Next time, you can give that money to me that you spent on them lawyers. If all it takes is getting you to sign a check for six hundred or eleven hundred dollars. And not show up for court, and not do anything once I get there. Hell, I can do that. You were basically paying them for the title of 'attorney', right?" Woo joked.

"Yeah, girl, you're right," I sighed.

The sad thing about her joke was she was telling the gospel truth.

{ CHAPTER 9 }

It's True That When It Rains It Also Pours

In addition to my legal woes, I had to be concerned about one of my rental properties. I'd had no luck finding a tenant for this single-family home. There was no way in hell that I could pay two mortgages. So, I saw this coming and I decided to list it before I got behind on the payments. The property was listed for ninety days. At least, that's what I thought. Billy, my co-worker who was helping me to sell the property, was acting as my agent. He didn't reduce the price of the property in the multiple listing services (MLS) to the price that the mortgage company had agreed on. He wanted the property for himself at the reduced price. It was called a short sale, which drastically reduced the selling price of a property in order to induce a rapid transaction. I found out what Billy was trying to pull off and stopped him, right in his tracks.

"Wait. Let me stop you right there. Why were you using a co-worker instead of a legitimate agent?" Woo asked. I could imagine the skeptical frown that was on her face.

"He was a legitimate agent. Hell, he had a license," I said. "Plus, I didn't think he was so shabby and low-down."

"Ok, think about it. Billie's primary vocation is with the postal service, right?"

"What's the point of that question?" I asked. I was getting a little agitated from the questioning for some reason.

"The point is you got a real estate agent who was a postal worker. It is what it is, Molly. Would you go to a dentist to get Botox shots or to a chef who did work on cars in his spare time?" Woo asked. "Unless he could say that both jobs were equal in how qualified he was to do them, he's gonna be doing one full time and the other part time. You could get a good result, but you could get a so-so result," Woo said. Once again, she was speaking nothing but the truth.

"I see what you're saying," I said.

"The thing is, if you need your car repaired, you don't get a hairstylist to do it," Woo said.

"Ok, Ok, I got it! Let me continue my story."

I had so much going on. I cried out to God asking Him to please help me, although it seemed like my pleas were falling on deaf ears. Maybe God was upset with me for my forsaking Him through using those occult practices. I was so confused. I asked God to please send me some answers. Maybe He had been all along, but for some reason I was deaf to His words. Had He heard my pleas? Maybe, it was me who was blocking the communication. I decided to start a fast to open my mind and soul to an answer from God. I had no food for three days.

Only liquids and my prayers were my sustenance. I was a total mess — fasting, crying, and praying.

I really wished I had either Cathy or Jay as my lawyers, but Cathy was only accepting criminal cases. I was far too embarrassed to go back to Jay once more. If I had only done the sensible thing and kept Jay in the beginning, I coulda spared myself a lot of time, trial, tribulation and heartache. Again, if I had judged the situation by my heart and intuition, rather than allowing flash and superficiality to rule; the outcome would have completely different. It was clear to me that I was my own worst enemy, at times.

I set up an appointment with this attorney by the name of Harry Zane. When I arrived at his office, a man was standing outside drinking a cup of coffee. I struck up a conversation since we were both waiting on Mr. Zane. I found out that this guy had been working with Zane for the past twelve years, as a private detective. Harry Zane seemed to have all I needed. This man was the real deal. When I met him, he was also quite a gentleman and so was the private investigator. I felt at home.

During our conversation, I wanted to be honest with Mr. Zane about everything. I told him about the grievances that I had filed on the other attorneys. I also told him exactly what happened with Del Joseph. After I had bared my soul to him, he said that he wasn't sure if he wanted the case. You shoulda seen the look on my face. It was as if I had fallen one number short of a winning lottery ticket. I wouldn't wish that level of sinking disappointment on anyone, short of Thomas. It was a horrible feeling. It was the same sensation one would feel if the love of his life left him for another.

When I left his office, I was feeling so down. I mustered up enough strength to make myself get on the internet. I spent twelve damn hours that day searching for another attorney. I was so damn tired. Zane told me before I left his office that he would think it over during the weekend. He said that he wanted to make sure of some things and check some things out. I presumed he meant me. It wasn't looking good for me. It was hard to find an attorney. I had four thousand dollars to spend on representation and no attorney wanted to take my case.

{ CHAPTER 10 }

What Can A Bad Girl Do To Be Good?

My friend Kena, whose real name is Samantha, called while all this was going on. She wanted to spend some time with me. So, I met her up the street from my home at a restaurant. She followed me back to my house. I was so glad to see her. Hell, I needed someone to talk to. I needed the stress released from my mind and body. Kena could really relieve some of the pressure, particularly from a sexual aspect. There were a couple of things I didn't like about Kena, though. She wasn't only a cocaine head, but she was smoking weed and cigarettes. Kena was pretty and fine as hell, but she was so messed up. Kena's beauty made up for most of the discomfort of being around her vices. We spent the entire day and night together. We had sex off and on for nearly two days. We paused only to eat and sleep a little. Then, we got right back at it. We were screwing all over my condo, from room to room, on the floor, or wherever the feeling moved us.

Kena wanted me to fuck her with the strap-on dildo. She wanted me to use it twice in that day and I did. On the second go-around, I smelt burnt rubber. I look down to see that a piece of the dildo had melted. That's when I remembered what my old friend Sidney said years ago. He would always say, "I want some hot young pussy." I never really understood the connotation until then. Kena's pussy was the hottest that I had encountered in my life! Older women who I had been with were either cold or lukewarm in comparison. Hell, sex with Summer was great, but it couldn't compare with Kena's hot ass pussy.

Now, as I'm thinking about her, I can remember how it felt to have her stimulate me from the back. Kena would have her hands creeping underneath my shirt to fondle my 34 D breasts. My nipples would be as hard as rocks. She was good at circling my nipples with her fingertips as her soft lips touched my neck. She pressed her hot breasts against my back sending an electric impulse up my spine.

"Molly, shut the hell up! I always knew your hot little ass had a screw loose. You're wild as hell," Woo laughed.

"Yup, I'm a sex fiend. You know my story now. I've been trying to get your pretty ass, but you won't give me none," I joked

"Naw, you know I like "real" hard dicks. You can get off my jock now and resume your story please," Woo said with mock disdain.

A couple of days passed, I was still calling different attorneys. Finally, I received a call from Harry Zane. He said that he didn't sleep at all Saturday night, because he was thinking about my case. He said that he had mentioned me to his wife over dinner and had asked her what she thought. Zane said his wife told him to go with his heart. He said that he kept having dreams of me and him in a court room, but we were before a different judge. Zane said his wife asked him, what was wrong and why he kept waking up. He told her that he kept dreaming dreams, one after another, about my case. That's when he told me to come over to his office in the next hour. He had decided that he was going to take my case.

He asked, "So, what do you think about the dreams and my decision?"

I said, "I think that God has answered my prayers, Mr. Zane."

I got dressed, kissed Kena good-bye, and headed for the highway. I made it to his office in less than an hour. We went over all of the parameters of the case. I was pleased. Even though, I was fourteen thousand dollars in the red over this case, at least there was some light at the end of the tunnel. Mr. Zane was the answer to my prayers. I felt so comfortable in his office and with his staff.

He charged me thirty seven hundred. I had thirty days to answer the counter suit. Del Joseph had fucked my case up by giving that two week extension. Why did his dumb ass get a verbal commitment? He should have gotten all of it documented. It was the professional thing to do. If he had cared any thing about me or my case, he woulda taken the time to get all of the settlement parameters in writing.

It was crystal clear that Del Joseph only cared about getting that eleven hundred dollars out of me, as a payment for filing the suit in superior court. He thought that this method would be a simple and effective scare tactic against the opposing attorney. He tried to force an agreement, since no attorney really wants to waste time in court. Del Joseph gambled on that fact. He woulda been successful, if he had simply gotten the agreement in writing.

A couple of weeks passed. I got a notice from Zane stating that I had to appear in court for mediation. I called him to inquire. He didn't return my call. I got another notice from him a week later, indicating that the mediation was put off for two weeks. Weeks went by and Zane still hadn't returned my calls. I continued to pray and hope that he hadn't gotten caught up in Thomas's and his attorney's lies. I wondered incessantly why Zane didn't return my calls.

{ CHAPTER 11 }

The Deliberation

I broke down and went to Mrs. Tex. I asked her to come over to my house and do an absolution. Mrs. Tex came over and blessed my home. She sprinkled me with holy water and oils. I had gone to all extremes, from voodoo to the power of the Bible. Maybe I was serving two masters in doing so, but that was not my intention. I was suffering and I was seeking relief. I wanted to be free of the spirits that had been tormenting me for all these years.

"What's an absolution?" Woo asked.

"This is when the negative influences that are around and possibly in the home of a person are driven away, sort of like an exorcism."

"How long did this take?" Woo asked.

"The deliberation lasted five hours."

We burned all of the oils, candles, parchment paper, voodoo dolls, essentially anything affiliated with the practice of voodoo. All remnants of my trip to Marie Laveau's grave were thrown out. It was gone, never to return. I had turned from God by soliciting the help of occult practitioners, which was clearly something that was forbidden in Christianity. My circumstances didn't improve, but the severity was magnified. I should not have doubted God or questioned His methods. I was anxious. I lacked faith and conviction. As a result, my turning to voodoo had cost me. I can't help but to think about the thousands that I spent on voodoo. There were no effective results. Why would I have doubted God, who had protected me and who had granted me the nine lives of a cat? I sat back and pondered my situation. I came to the valid conclusion that, most of the time, I was a victim of my own circumstances. None of this was coincidental. It was all avoidable, if I had only followed my God-given instincts.

****

I finally got around to writing up my complaint to the real-estate commission against Billy. I found out that it was a six month process. In other words, the real-estate commission was six months behind. Now, I found out that, not only are there unethical attorneys, but there are unethical real estate agents and brokers.

"Molly, I'm curious to know if the commissions are finding these agents accountable for their actions," Woo stated.

"Hopefully, they're not like the bar association 'cause if they are I might have to protest," I said. "I'm sick and tired of this shit."

"I think the problem is, you have people in high positions who are elected officials and they have friends who they look out for. It's called the "good ol' boy" system," Woo said angrily.

"Yeah, many of them are making six figure salaries and they ain't doing shit," I replied. "They're not holding these unscrupulous people accountable. In many cases, they're taking money under the table."

During the fiasco which led to my property being auctioned, I had yet another improbable event which has so marked my life. A "reverend" by the name of Yarbrook had been trying to purchase the property, but he couldn't secure financing. This song and dance between us went on for three months, until I was finally forced to go through Billy. I inexplicably received a call from Reverend Yarbrook during the time of the foreclosure.

"Molly, I was just calling you about the property," he said. "I'm going to put in a bid for it, because I know that it's in foreclosure."

"How did you know the property was in foreclosure?" I asked.

"The lawyer who is handling the proceedings called me," he said sheepishly

"Why in the world would he tell you anything about my property?" I asked defiantly.

"Well, when we were talking about me buying the property, I went down to the courthouse and attached a thirty eight thousand dollar lien on it," he said rather matter-of-factly.

I was livid at this point. At this level of anger, I could have done anything.

"How in the hell can you go to the courthouse and put a lien on a property that you haven't put a damn dime into? You ain't no damn reverend. You're a crook!"

"Well, I thought at that time it was a done deal."

"Here I was thinking that I had to worry about Billy's black ass. Now, I have to worry about your crooked black monkey ass, too!" I shouted into the phone.

"I just put a lien on the property, because we had an agreement that I would buy it."

Yarbrook, "That was like five fucking months ago! Your damn ass couldn't get financed. You got your fucking nerve putting a lien on a property that you hadn't put one cent of blood, sweat, and tears into. That shit you did was illegal and I'm gonna get to the bottom of this," I said as I slammed down the phone.

Reverend Yarbrook was nothing but a wolf dressed in sheep's clothing. How can anyone just go down to the courthouse and file a lien on someone's property having never done any type of work on it? This was bullshit! One thing was for sure, this wasn't the first time Yarbrook had done something like this.

"While we're on the subject of real estate, what happened to your condo at Mahogany Square? I loved that place. It was beautiful," Woo said.

"Oh, I never told you what happened with that condo?" I asked.

"Hell, you hadn't told me anything about you based on what you are spilling tonight!"

"Yeah, I guess you're right. Well, I lost it to Vesta Holdings," I said.

"How in the world could that happen? You were big balling back then!"

"Are you sure that you want to hear this now? There's not much to it," I said.

"Why don't you let me be the judge of that, Miss Thang?"

"Ok, then, remember when I had six rooming houses? Well, I didn't have an escrow account on any of the mortgages, not even on my condo. The problem started when I forgot to pay twenty two hundred dollars of property taxes on that condo. Vesta Holdings then swooped in and bid those twenty two hundred dollars all the way up to one hundred and ten thousand!" I fumed.

"Nuh uh, that can't be for real!" Woo said.

"Yes, hell, they did do that shit! It was the county's fault, because they were very slow recording deeds after closing. It wasn't showing up on their records that I had a mortgage!" I said.

"That's how you lost the condo? That's pure bullshit!"

"Well, I didn't want it to happen. True enough I forgot to pay the taxes, but them sorry ass bastards at the county contributed to it," I said.

"That was dirty, Molly. That's the kind of crap that they do to elderly people."

"Yes, Ma'am. That was dirty, but I survived it and I even prospered a little."

"How did you manage that?" Woo asked.

"After everything was over, I ended up walking away with eighty five thousand dollars free and clear. I surrendered the condo and Vesta Holdings was stuck with an unknown mortgage of one hundred and thirty thousand dollars. It was one year later that Vesta found out that I had gotten their eighty five thousand out of the escrow account for the purchase," I said.

"So, in all of this, it seems like the angels were looking out for you, or maybe it was the devil," Woo quipped.

"Nope, that was my guardian angels looking out for me. I

was treated wrongly and things were made right. I need to listen to and see what they keep trying to show me instead of doing the opposite things sometimes," I said.

"Molly, I bet you have made your guardian angels cry a thousand times during your life," Woo said with a voice that was now strangely serious.

"I can't say that you are wrong about that. The only thing I can do from this day forward is to try to make them laugh instead of cry, I guess," I said with a smile on my face that Woo couldn't see, but she could certainly hear loudly and clearly.

{ CHAPTER 12 }

Mediation

I had called Harry Zane twice and he didn't return my calls either time. I can only think back to the day that I was in his office. He was so nice. He asked his staff to come into his office to meet me. He told them that I was a "special" client. He made me feel good about myself and the case. I thought that he really and truly cared about me. As it turned out, he only cared about getting the thirty seven hundred dollar fee from me, justifying it as being twenty-two billable hours. He said that even if we had to do depositions that it wouldn't take twenty two hours. When we got to mediation, Thomas's attorney told the mediator, Helen Carter-Weber, that they were not willing to mediate, yet they were prepared to do depositions.

Every thing was preplanned. The reason that I firmly believe this is because I remembered what had transpired when I walked upstairs the day of mediation. Harry Zane was speaking with a deputy at that time. He stopped the conversation briefly to say to me with a stern look, "Go and sit in the mediation room and I will be there in a minute."

One would think that with Zane being my attorney and knowing that I had called him twice in a month without so much as a return call, the minimum greeting that would be appropriate would be a smile. His greeting to me was as neutral as one of those guards at Buckingham Palace. I went to the mediation room. After sitting in there for twenty minutes, in walked ol' green-eyed Wellman, Thomas and his two trained puppets, Britney and Tracey.

I heard the clerk say, "The other party's attorney is not here."

Attorney Wellman said, "Yes he is. He's in the hallway. I just saw him. I'll go get him."

Suddenly, it all dawned on me. Wellman knew Zane and they had pre-arranged every damn thing. I was all alone again. I was about to be bamboozled once more. They had met and they had talked and it was painfully obvious. When we were put in separate rooms, Zane made it look as though he was making an offer to settle for twenty percent of what the value of the modeling agency was. In his opinion, it was valued at around ten thousand dollars. I explained to the mediator what was going on. I tried to warn her about Thomas and how he lied so well. When Mrs. Weber went into the other room, Zane asked me if I had the money to pay for the mediation, which was two hundred fifty dollars.

I said to him, "I thought that it was coming out of the thirty seven hundred."

He said, "No."

I said, "Well, I will have to send you a check."

He was visibly upset, but he happened to have a blank check in his wallet. He took it out and filled it out. He had taken thirty seven hundred dollars from me just to go to mediation. This was unheard of. Even Georgia's top attorneys would not have charged that much for something as simple as mediation. I was advised by both Zane and Mrs. Weber that the outcome would probably have been the same if I had gone to trial or come to a mutual agreement. I was advised that going to trial would cost me even more money and it was best that both parties mutually agreed to dismiss.

The result of this would be that neither I, nor the defendant would have rights to the modeling agency. When we left, Zane told Wellman, "Just come by the office and pick up an original copy of the agreement." Once Zane and I walked out the court room, we were surrounded by at least three potential clients. Each looked at me, gauging my level of satisfaction with Zane as their eyes said that they needed an attorney. I tried to convey to them with my eyes that they should keep looking. As I got ready to leave, I turned to Zane and I looked at him with a stare of resignation and disappointment.

He asked me, "When is your birthday?"

I replied, "August."

"Don't worry about sending me a check. I'll let that be your birthday gift."

I smiled and walked away.

"That dude Zane sounded like a pussy-assed lawyer," Woo said.

"Woo, he seemed so different until he got my money. In fact, they all acted differently before and after the money. Customer service in the legal industry is lacking as far as I'm concerned. I went through more lawyers with that Thomas bullshit than most people see in a lifetime and what did it get me?" I said.

"Molly, maybe you should stop judging the book by its cover, and maybe you should read a few pages before you buy the book. When you go to a bookstore, do you just pick up a book that looks good and buy it? Hell, Naw! You read ten to twelve pages or maybe even a chapter, if you have the time. That's the way we should judge people, but most of us go by the pretty cover and we end up buying a sorry-ass, boring as hell book. By that time it's too late," Woo stated.

"That point is well taken. Preach on, sista girl!" I joked.

{ CHAPTER 13 }

You Can't Outrun Your Past

Finally, I managed to get a copy of the court documents concerning statements from Maggie in Thomas's order against Phyllis. After months of fighting the spirit of depression and thanks to the prayers and the deliberation by Ms. Tex. I got up enough strength to go down to the county court house and look through Thomas's entire file. I sat down at the counter and read the entire thing. Afterwards, I made copies of all his files. Twenty five cents a copy was not a problem, but it was difficult to sit there and read all the lies this man had gotten away with. It was like reading a novel by the world's greatest con artist.

Thomas beat the system by appearing to be the victim in all of his claims, and they were all basically the same. He claimed in each case that he felt frightened for his life and that of his family's. He claimed to be afraid of Phyllis. He said that she would kill him. That was the basis of the protective order against her and the reason why she was put in jail. He even accused Phyllis of trying to molest Barry. What did he have to gain by saying that this child was a victim of a sexual assault? I wanted to cry, but I held back my tears. I began to feel flush in the face, but held back until I got in the car where the floodgates were opened. I truly felt for these people who Thomas had hurt both physically and emotionally. Now, I had to confront Maggie. I went to the job and waited on Maggie until it was time for her shift to begin. She arrived within an hour. I showed her the letter that she said she knew nothing of.

Maggie said, "This is my signature, but I didn't write the letter." She claimed that she had never seen the letter.

I said, "Maggie, this letter has your original signature on it and it's on record. Surely, you would not have signed something without reading it. Did you know that this letter had Phyllis locked up and taken away from her son for seven months?"

Maggie didn't utter a sound. The look on her face was that of a person who had seen someone from her past who had come back to hunt her down.

"Well, if you didn't write the letter, will you be willing to go down to the court house and tell them that?" I asked.

"I—I have too much on my plate, right now," Maggie stammered.

I am so glad that my co-workers Bonnie, Mrs. Hall, Mrs. Moldon, and Mark all knew about the situation. They all heard Maggie say that Thomas gave Phyllis a massive overdose of Ibuprofen to the tune of 12,000 milligrams in a twenty-four hour period. Now, it will not be my word against hers.

Maggie then said, "I'll give a sworn statement, if Phyllis's family got an attorney and subpoenaed me to appear in court as a witness."

Now, I am beginning to think that Maggie may have in some way assisted Thomas. I don't want to think that, but everything leads me to believe that possibility, especially after reading that horrible letter that she wrote for Thomas to corroborate his lie against Phyllis.

Now, I stand in no man's land, a purgatory which lies between truth and morality. Maybe I have lived my life as a model in legions, a good thought which never materialized into what it should have been. There is always another day, I tell myself, and the only thing I hate is waiting for this one to turn the page. I won't even think about it. I'll just dream about how happy I will be tomorrow.

{ CHAPTER 14 }

The Prize That I Have Chased For My Entire Life

"Whew! That was one hell of a story. I feel like I've lived your life. I know so much about you. Damn, you have lived some kind of life. Molly. You could tell a lot of people a lot of stuff 'bout how to deal with people. You've done it all as far as I can see," Woo said.

"I've done a lot of shit, been with a lot of people, and seen a lot of things. I've lived two lifetimes it seems to me sometimes," I sighed.

It was daylight outside. Woo and I had been talking for eleven hours, but it seemed like four. We had begun talking around 8:30 the previous night and now it was 7:45 in the morning. I had given Woo the bullet-points version of a complicated life and it felt refreshing, as though I had purged my soul of some bile or venom that was making me spiritually sick.

"You know what, Woo. There's something else that I didn't say, so since I've been baring my soul to you, I might as well tell it all," I said.

"You might as well since you have told me everything else about you," Woo said.

"Okay, this one is hard, but, hell, it shouldn't be. It's kinda silly that I am hesitant about telling you this, but here goes. With all of the men and women that I've been with, I had never had an orgasm once," I said.

"Get the fuck out of here, Molly. You're lying!" Woo said, with a tone that was laced with total shock. "How many people have you been with that you can recall?" she asked.

"When Mrs. Tex did her deliberation on me in my condo. She had me to write down the names of all of the people I had sex with on a piece of paper to be torn up and stomped on. Before it could even reach the tearing phase, it had taken forever. I had written the names of over two-hundred men and women and some of them I couldn't even remember. Mrs. Tex looked at me as if to say, 'How many damn names could you have for it to take this fucking long?'"

At first, Woo laughed for about a minute. After she finished, she asked, "So, with over two-hundred men and women, not one of them even came close to making you cum?"

"It's true, strange as it may seem. To give you an example, with the men, it would be exciting to do everything, the kissing and fondling. I would be aroused right up until they penetrated me and then it would be nothing at all, ZERO. It was much better with women as I loved the softness and everything that made a female a female. Even though I loved women, I still could not climax with them. Although, the sex itself was still enjoyable," I said.

"So, you have NEVER had an orgasm is what you are telling me?" Woo asked.

"I never said that."

"Okay, now you're playing games. Have you or haven't you ever had an orgasm?"

"Yes. I have, but it wasn't until this year that it happened. A friend was having one of those parties that are really meant for you to buy something. This was not a Tupperware party, but a sex toy party where you buy dildos, vibrators, edible panties or anything that you wanted. I was told that if I wanted to experience an out of this world orgasm that I should try this egg-shaped vibrator. I bought it and I used it that night. I had my first orgasm and it was so fantastic! It was as if I was falling off of the earth. I felt the vibrations inside of me. They were like waves of pleasure and explosions. The orgasms felt so wonderful that I started crying. I think that maybe my whole life has been my pursuing this little bit of Heaven on Earth. Now that I have the vibrator, I don't feel the need to have female companionship. If it comes, fine. If not, I know how to cum on my own now," I joked.

"Girl, you are so silly, but I see where you're coming from," Woo said.

"Hey, girlfriend. It's been good talking with you tonight or rather today. I feel like the weight of the world has been lifted from my shoulders. Sometimes, you just need to talk with another person, instead of keeping stuff bottled up. A talk is as good as seeing a psychiatrist sometimes."

"Hell, yeah! Most of the time all they do is listen to you talk and then charge your ass like a hundred dollars an hour. Okay, you owe me twelve hundred dollars and I expect my check to be in the mail," Woo joked.

"Don't you hold your damn breath waiting for that check, 'cause it probably ain't showing up. In fact, it's a 100% probability that hell would freeze over first," I said

Woo and I laughed for two minutes before anyone had the energy to speak again.

"See, that comment probably made your guardian angel laugh," Woo said.

"So, do I really owe you anything other than my eternal gratitude?"

"This one is a freebie, but the next time, it's gonna cost you. I can't eat or buy shit if I pay with gratitude."

We laughed again but not as long as before.

"Thank you, Dr. Woo. Have a good morning," I said as I hung up my phone.

{ CHAPTER 15 }

Looking At The Road Through The Rear View Mirror

Life to me is not like a box of chocolates, life is a Pandora's Box filled with "what if's". It doesn't matter how rich you are or how poor you are, you going to go through hell in some form or fashion unless you are just plain lucky. This is why you have to say "thank you, God" on the days that you are sitting there and you notice how peaceful your surroundings are. You notice that all your bills are paid and you have some spending money in your pocket. I should have been saying that right before I met Thomas, but I let satan enter into my life to create doubt and depression. It was the holidays and yes we grieve over loved ones the most during this time, but "what if" I had been home with the rest of my family over in Alabama. Instead I alienated myself by, not answering the phone and crying my eyes out. I was torturing myself through the denial of my emotions.

Some people believe that life is predetermined from birth. I don't believe that in the least. I believe that we ARE our choices and we live our decisions. Why would God pre-destine me to be homosexual, decide before I was born that I would suffer the assaults to my physical and mental well-being, or make the decision for me to have sex with over two hundred people? The directions that we take are not forced upon us by God, but are paths that we choose on our own and whatever the result, good or bad, right or wrong are directly related to those choices. All of my life it has seemed as though it has been one thing after another to torment me. I know that sometimes I brought things on myself by not thinking before acting. Other times, shit just came blowing my way and I was an innocent bystander. I could have eliminated so much stress in my life, if I had heeded my guardian angels. As I look back, if I had only remembered the times before when I was rescued right in the nick of time then I would have realized that the angels were there. I would have thought about my actions before I proceeded. With careful consideration, I could have foreseen the ramifications of what I had planned to do before I moved forward with that plan. If I had simply kept to the road less traveled that God had laid out for me, then I most assuredly would have escaped the horrors that I have suffered over the years.

Always, there are days that I forget to say my prayers and thank God for his mercy on my harried soul. There are nights when I get into the bed without kneeling and thanking him for putting my one foot before the other and bringing me home safely. One thing I now know is that, I was watched over throughout my life more than I knew at the time that he was protecting me.

Some might ask how I can speak about my life and homosexuality, while in the same breath speaking of God. The simple answer is the honest one. I didn't make me, God did, and it was for a specific reason. I didn't choose my sexuality any more than I chose my race or the color of my eyes. It was an act of nature, the universe or anything else other than an unborn combination of my mother's egg and my father's sperm fertilized and implanted in my mother's womb. I am not trying to talk about homosexuality in a negative or positive sense, but in a factual way. I am what and who I am. I honestly cannot fight off the desire that I have for women. I believe that God loves us for our hearts and not because of something that one has absolutely no choice over. My sexuality IS me and no amount of prayers or interventions can change my biological makeup.

What if, I had hidden my sexuality and forced myself to live a lie based upon society's social codes? Would I be married with a house filled with kids, become a housewife, staying home to cook and clean and still have to sneak and be with a woman? I would have become a "Housewife Lesbian," as was the case with so many of the hundred or so women I slept with, who openly denied any homosexual feelings toward another female, yet who were more than willing to have sex with me in private. No, to do so would have meant that I would be living a lie. The worst person in the world that you can ever lie to, is yourself. I can say this with all conviction, even though I was married twice. No, because I am a Lesbian and I am not ashamed of what I was created to be.

With all this suffering sometimes we forget the most important thing. We've forgotten how to love each other, but most importantly we've forgotten how to love ourselves. I have learned to love Molly, unconditionally. The problem was that I never really knew Molly, as I grew up. It has taken me years to discover this, but she is really a wonderful person. I was too busy trying to get more and then more of whatever it was, be it money, women or whatever the case, to really discover who I am. I had to learn the hard way about being greedy with a mop stick struck across my ass, when I could have listened to my inner self and I could have spared such a lesson. I have learned and lost so much from my mistakes that I honestly cannot afford to make any of them ever again. I could keep on making the same thoughtless choices as before and ultimately end up on a trash heap, but I have learned to listen to the angels, to laugh with them over the happiness of a sensible venture with good intentions, rather than sharing tearful moments lamenting yet another bad decision. Thank God for keeping me alive! Committing suicide was surely not the answer to my problems, and though I tried, I now realize that act would have been one of cowardice. I may be a lot of things, but I am no coward.

If I had a chance to live my life over, what would I do differently? I would have never gone to that dance club that night, for sure. I would have never had either abortion. I probably wouldn't have had so many sex partners. I most certainly would have never tried to kill myself. I would have transferred to Marionville instead of Valletta. I would have never put so much blind trust in people without taking the time to really know them. I would have never gotten married so fast and so many times. The most important change is that, I would have never doubted God! I did and I can see clearly where my doubts left me, on satan's doorstep filled with grief. "Tell the truth and shame the Devil" is an old saying that I have put into action through my open baring of my soul.

What will be the outcome of such revelations? Will Thomas be brought to justice for murdering Phyllis? Probably not, since Phyllis's family has closed the book on her life despite the facts that I revealed to them. I do know that Karma will eventually exact its perfect revenge on Thomas. I am sure of this. I can only hope that exposing my life in such a bare and explicit way that someone will understand the value of honesty, honor and truth in dealing with others, something I didn't understand until I had many years of reflection. I honestly can say that I put the material before the spiritual many times in my life and I brought tears to my guardian angels. Now, we rejoice over my triumphs and the angels still shed tears. The difference is that now those tears are tears of joy!

Phyllis, your story has been told as a part of mine. Now, the truth of what happened has been revealed to anyone who chooses to care. Whatever happens from this point forward will be determined by the universe. You are no longer bound to me and you are free to go, to move into that eternal light of unconditional love. Yes, it is time for you to find your peace in God's paradise. I only ask one favor of you once you get there, and that is for you to say hello to Mazie Bell for me.

ACKNOWLEDGEMENTS

I would like to start by thanking my new friend, Kenneth Barlow. Without you, I could have never completed this novel. Thank you, Ken, for all the late night hours and sweat poured into this book. Thank you so much for being a friend and not judging me at all. God placed you in my life and I thank him so much everyday for such.

Mr. Barlow is a published author who resides in Atlanta, GA. His book is called "Dr. Keenan's Fat Loss Solution". He can be contacted at kkbarlow@hotmail.com.

I want to say "thank you" to everyone who has ever helped me throughout the years in any kind of way—especially, those of you who never turned a deaf ear—"I never Forgot Yaw!"

Thanks to Dr. B. Prince, Dr. John W. Ross, Dr. C. Beal, Dr. U. Ujah, Dr. Johns, Dr. Hubbell, Dr. Mullins, Dr. J. Blount, Dr. Abassi, Dr. K. Robinson, Dr. Nate Grady, Dr. Gwendolyn Goldsby Grant, Attorney D. Belgrave, Attorney P. Sanchez, Levenson & Associates, and Attorney Alterman,

Thanks to my special friends: QDANGEROUS, Brandi

Neal, Charles Bowers, Ralph Brown-Local 32, Flanagan, Ben Patterson, Odonyo Bowen, Michael McCatty, Mr. Danny Brantley, Mrs. Blackshear, Nathan, Johnny Weaver, Cecil Johnson, Assuanta Collins, Windy Goodloe, Steven F. Turner, Crystal White, Marva & Jozef Pikula, "DJ", T.Manning, Maude Tyler-Clayborn, S. Dunn, Marshall Burton, Tony Dunn, Kim Nelson., Wanda Flanagan, Tre'Lane, Tammy Williams, Diane, Marilyn Gainey, Marie Kennedy, Rozena W., Fran-che', Peter & Paul & Carlos @ Shop 71, Mike @ Jakki Colours, B. Brooks, Gino, W. Powell, Shay, Wayne Smith, "GG", Bobby & Amanda Johnson, Mr. Woods, Mr. P. Black, T. Roebuck, Pebbles, "K".

I thank God for being the second person in the FIRE!! I was bound hand and feet.

My thoughts were filled with doubt. "God, if you don't save me, I'm going under,"

I kept repeating!! I forgot so quickly that He said "I will never leave you nor forsake you." My faith was tested. God placed me in the FIRE and He showed up just in time.

All the time, I had the spirit of FEAR trying to control me, but Jesus said FEAR NOT?

He used those two words the most in the Bible and I forgot about the words. I forgot about the times before when he showed up just in time. God forgive me and cleanse my heart from all iniquities. I love you my heavenly father... I love you so much!!

I would like to thank my family, especially the ones who believed in me (you know who you are)!! To all my nieces and nephews "Yup" At last count there were forty- four of you guys (this includes greats) 'keep um coming!" I will need one of you guys to take care of me when I'm old, HA! HA! Don't think I never think about you guys. I think about you all the time even the ones I didn't watch grow up, "Yes, auntie thought about you all the time, even till this day." Bottom line—I love you so very much. I honestly live and breathe for you guys. You are my heart. I want to make you proud to say "that's my auntie"!!

Special thanks to Chris Krok, 750 AM for keeping me entertained.

I have to give a big shout out to Video, Buck aka Ron, P-Slim, Bev. Hood, Elaine Hart, Sheree M., Willie Harris, Paul Price, R.L., Jerry, Angie D., Pon Killens, Mike Nodine, Raheem, Val Johnson, Jacquelyn Holden-Johnson, Eric R, S. Redding, Sheryl Woods, David Jackson, Gladys Miller, Sil Johnson, Chappell, Nelson, T. Thomas, Mrs. Carolyn, Philip Reed, S. Hammond, Angie Davis, J. Harper, C. Andrews, Mrs. L. Texador, C. Clay, L. Washington, Lana Jones, D. Black, Jack Watson, C. Oronzio, J. Albano, T. Norman, Freeman, Donna Porter, Dot Tedder, S. Thompson, Tammy T., Glenda and Ervin Chapman, Shaw.

Also, all my ex-co-workers back at the West Palm Bch. GMF. I especially want to thank all of the men on the dock, particularly Randy and Ron & the truck drivers (LOL), and last the entire 030 crew.

If I miss any co-workers, it wasn't intentional. I want you all to know—if it wasn't for you guys, I don't think I could have made it these 21 long years. It was always a pleasure to see and speak with you all—you kept my mind off my troubles. You put many smiles on my face when I was sad. Thank you,

I love you guys for real!

There are so many people that supported me, I'm sure I'm going to leave a name out.

If I offended anyone, I do apologize!

If I left anyone out, I'll get you on the next book.

I have to thank the book clubs and authors who have supported me and My Toastmaster's family.

Also the book store owners and the booksellers: Thank you

My readers: who make it all especially worthwhile?

And last, my little girl, MaryBell.

I told you guys, "I'm writing a book, HA!"

Again, thank you all for your support... THANK YOU ... for everything.

www.ingramcontent.com/pod-product-compliance
Lightning Source LLC
Chambersburg PA
CBHW030240170426
43202CB00007B/65